Dick

Dick

The Man Who Is President

John Nichols

THE NEW PRESS

NEW YORK
LONDON

Requests for permission to reproduce selections from this book should be mailed to:
Permissions Department, The New Press, 38 Greene Street, New York, NY 10013

Published in the United States by The New Press, New York, 2004
Distributed by W. W. Norton & Company, Inc., New York

ISBN 1-56584-840-3 (hc)
CIP data available

The New Press was established in 1990 as a not-for-profit alternative to the large,
commercial publishing houses currently dominating the book publishing industry. The
New Press operates in the public interest rather than for private gain, and is committed
to publishing, in innovative ways, works of educational, cultural, and community value
that are often deemed insufficiently profitable.

www.thenewpress.com

Composition by dix!

Printed in the United States of America

10   9   8   7   6   5   4   3   2   1

CONTENTS

CONTENTS

THE EVIL GENIUS IN THE CORNER

Am I the evil genius in the corner that nobody ever sees come out of his hole? It's a nice way to operate, actually.

—Vice President Richard Cheney, January 2004

The suspicion that every serious observer of Washington comings and goings had entertained for months was finally confirmed three weeks after George Bush and Dick Cheney took their oaths of office. Throughout the fall presidential campaign of 2000, Bush had struggled gamely, if not gracefully, to assume the front-man role to which he had been assigned by his family and their retainers. The least articulate Republican presidential nominee since Calvin Coolidge, and the least practically prepared standard-bearer in the party's history, Bush toured the land—as a prince whose only qualification to lead the party of Lincoln, or to hold the office once occupied by Washington was his lineage. Defeated soundly in the popular voting of his countrymen and -women, Bush was installed in the White House only by a Supreme Court majority that had been selected by administrations in which his father served. George W. was inaugurated on January 20, 2001, delivering a vapid inaugural address that begged the question: How could this son of privilege, who had avoided responsibility most of his adult life, run four businesses into the ground, and floated through a political career crafted and controlled by the ministers and minions of his father, former president George Herbert Walker Bush, presume to lead the most powerful and complex government ever assembled by man?

The answer came at 11:30 A.M. on February 7, 2001, when a suicidal accountant from Evansville, Indiana, wandered up to the wrought-iron fence along the South Lawn of the White House and aimed a handgun toward the presidential residence. Robert W. Pickett, who a week earlier had sent a suicide note to the commissioner of the Internal Revenue Service, and who described himself in letters to newspaper editors as "a victim of a corrupt government," was apparently trying to commit suicide by cop when he fired several rounds from a .38-caliber revolver in the direction of the White House. It didn't work. A member of the White House emergency response team shot Pickett in the knee, and within moments he was taken into custody.

Following established procedure, however, the White House was sealed off almost as soon as Pickett began shooting. Unaware of whether or not a terrorist incident was playing out, Secret Service agents rushed to the sides of the vice president and president. They found Cheney working on a speech in his office in the West Wing, surrounded by ringing phones, a buzzing computer, and scurrying aides—the image of a CEO, in charge and hard at work on a Wednesday morning barely two weeks after assuming a new and demanding position.

They found George Bush in the White House gym. He was working out. And why not? He had no real responsibilities. He was president in name only. Dick Cheney was in charge.

George Walker Bush may hold the title of commander in chief. But the power was, and is, in the hands of Richard Bruce

Cheney, a shadowy Zelig figure who has spent the better part of four decades quietly proving the truth of Oliver Wendell Holmes's observation that "the only prize much cared for by the powerful is power." Cheney achieved his power the old-fashioned way: he clawed and connived, capitulated and compromised, enough so that, finally, the dominant economic, military, and political interests that guide the United States, and by extension the world, became convinced that he could be trusted with the keys to the kingdom.

Cheney did not rise on the basis of his competence, as the official spin would have it.

His career has been characterized by dashed hopes, damaging missteps, and dubious achievements. No, it was not competence; rather, Cheney has climbed the ladder of success because of his willingness, proven again and again, to sacrifice principle and the public good in the service of his own ambition and of those who might advance it.

Cheney, whose Wizard of Oz–like penchant for remaining behind the curtains of authority has always been so pronounced that Secret Service agents once code-named him "Backseat," possesses a résumé that would by any traditional measure qualify him for the presidency: aide to three chief executives, the youngest White House chief of staff in American history, the second most powerful member of his party in the House of Representatives, cabinet secretary, CEO of a powerful and politically connected corporation. But what made Cheney so appealing to so many of those who pull and push the levers of power was his record of loyalty to men who did not deserve it, to policies that had not worked, and to fantasies of global rule entertained only by the most drastically deluded megalomaniacs. By the time he reached middle age, Cheney had personally seen one Republican presidency collapse into the impeachment process and protected another from that fate. He had managed a presidential campaign to narrow defeat and learned the tricks of avoiding that fate in the future. He had guided the country into war. He had diverted the post–cold war "peace dividend" back into a military-industrial complex that would replace containment and détente with preemptive war and global policing on an unprecedented scale. He had laid the groundwork for the "Contract with America" themes that would reshape the domestic politics of the nation and then handed over the project to Newt Gingrich for completion. Dick Cheney had been proximate to power for so long that he knew where all the bodies were buried. As is common with men who have had the experience of plotting political intrigues, preserving presidencies, and initiating wars, Cheney briefly entertained the prospect that he might rule not just in reality, but in name. However, the pretender's ambitions were dashed by the hard truths of politics in an age where image matters more than substance: he lacked the family ties, the aristocratic bearing, and the calculated charm that is required to be judged "presidential" in this time of television. So with the Bush family that he had long served coming again to power in 2001, Cheney settled for a role that in another time and country would have been dubbed "prince regent."

Understanding the subtleties of acquiring power better than any contemporary American political figure—including Henry Kissinger, whom a young Dick Cheney had bested in a White House war of wills during the administration of Gerald Ford—Cheney did what he had done since the start of his political career. While publicly declaring that his own time in the public sphere was done, Cheney artfully assumed a seemingly thankless task, that of identifying George W. Bush's running mate, and turned it to his own advantage. Playing upon the fears of the first President Bush that his son was ill prepared to be the second President Bush, Cheney presented himself as the solution: a baby-sitter vice president willing to relinquish the symbolism of the Oval Office for the satisfaction of complete control over the mechanisms of government. "Big changes are coming to Washington, and I want to be a part of it," Cheney noted blandly at the press conference where his selection was announced. Then, after grumbling out an acceptance speech at the 2000 Republican National Convention in Philadelphia, he disappeared.

Aside from a single tepid debate with the hapless Democratic nominee for vice president, Connecticut senator Joe Lieberman, Cheney placed himself on the political equivalent of the minor league baseball circuit, quietly touring second-tier towns to meet with carefully selected, invariably small audiences of Republican partisans. Weeks went by during which Cheney was barely mentioned in the national press. As election day approached, Cheney stepped further and further from the limelight, flying to smaller and smaller towns, attended by a dwindling crew of reporters who for the most part assumed that they had been assigned to political Siberia. The inattention served Cheney well, as he had little time for the demands of democracy. He was concerned not with the petty politics of electioneering, but with the real politics of power grabbing. After the Bush–Cheney ticket lost the popular vote for president by more than five hundred thousands ballots nationwide, Cheney played a pivotal role in pulling together the political team and the treasury that would disrupt the recounting of Florida ballots so thoroughly that, when the appropriate moment came, a Supreme Court dominated by his friend and hunting partner Antonin Scalia could "settle" the disputed election and make him the most powerful vice president in the nation's history.

During the interregnum, the vice president–in–waiting was preparing to return to Washington to run what, despite the official title, would in every sense be a Cheney-Bush administration. An increasingly disengaged George W. Bush admitted to reporters, in a rare moment of candor during the long wait for the court's intervention, that he would be more than happy to return to Texas if Al Gore secured the presidency. But Cheney displayed no such reticence. Even as the recounts and related legal battles of November and December 2000 progressed, Cheney dispatched himself to suburban Washington as head of the transition team that would shape the administration he knew would claim power in January.

While Bush busied himself fixing fences on his Texas ranchette, Cheney put in eighteen-hour days in a rented office where the next administration was taking shape. He had appointed himself chief of recruitment for the administration to come, and using the Rolodex he had been filling since he was a twenty-something congressional aide in the days when Lyndon Johnson occupied the White House, Cheney began piecing together not just a team, but a plan for remaking the United States, and the world, in an image more amenable to sixty-year-old white male CEOs. When Scalia closed down the Florida recount, it was not Bush but rather Cheney who stepped before the microphones in Washington to declare, "We will move as rapidly as we can to have a cabinet in place by the time of the inauguration. Expect the first announcement soon."

When the announcements began to come, one Cheney loyalist after another was awarded a perch in the hierarchy of the new administration. Cheney's co-conspirator from the Nixon and Ford administrations, Donald Rumsfeld, would run the Department of Defense. Paul Wolfowitz, who shared Cheney's fanatical fascination with preemptive war making, was installed in the number two position at the Pentagon. Secretary of State Colin Powell, the Washington super-survivor who could not be denied a role in the new administration that had benefited so greatly from his support during the campaign briefly assumed that he would have a role in shaping the new administration's foreign policies. But when he objected that placing the aggressively interventionist Wolfowitz in so pivotal a position would undermine the ability of the State Department to play its traditional leadership role in international relations, Powell soon found that neither he nor George W. Bush would be charting the nation's course in the world order. Cheney was in charge.

And if there was any doubt of that, Powell got the signal loud and clear when the vice president picked John Bolton, a militant unilateralist with an international reputation for disdaining the United Nations and other vehicles for multinational cooperation, to serve as undersecretary of state for arms control. Cheney put an old pal from the Ford administration, Alcoa CEO Paul O'Neill, in charge of the Department of the Treasury. And in the first of his many political favors to the religious Right, Cheney selected defeated Missouri senator John Ashcroft to serve as attorney general. But cabinet appointments were, for the most part, window dressing, as became evident when Cheney dismissed O'Neill for attempting to assert basic principles of economics and fiscal responsibility in a White House that was in official denial about the massive deficits it was creating—"a round peg in a square hole," griped Cheney in an interview with *USA Today* when he explained why he had fired his former friend.

In the most ideologically driven White House since that of Ronald Reagan, and in the most politically motivated White House since that of Richard Nixon, Cheney made himself the commissar. As O'Neill and other refugees from the administration revealed, he centralized the authority to make policy, distribute favors, and plot election strategy in the vice president's office to such an extent that it quickly became known that the meeting that mattered in this White House was with Cheney, not Bush. The president grew increasingly distant and disinterested—watching football games alone while choking down pretzels—as Cheney began charting the nation's energy policy in secret meetings with old business associates such as Enron's Ken Lay. Bush played the role of permanent candidate, jetting off to battleground states while Cheney governed. By the late summer of 2001, the White House political team that reported to Cheney was already worrying, a lot, about the coming anniversary of the November 7, 2000, election and the chaotic Florida recount that followed. "The anniversary of the Florida fiasco will find the survivor—Bush—in the swamp of a weak economy," wrote Howard Fineman in the edition of *Newsweek* magazine that appeared in the second week of September. Speculating that "doubts about Bush's legitimacy will resurface," Fineman wrote, "In the new-yet-old cold war, Florida is the DMZ, a rubble-strewn free-fire zone neither party can afford to lose. This week President Bush choppers in for two days with Jeb [Bush]." So it was that on the morning of September 11, 2001, Bush was seated on a child's stool at the Emma E. Booker Elementary School in

Sarasota, Florida, reading to the second graders in a classic campaign photo opportunity. Cheney was in the White House, conducting a morning meeting, when his secretary rushed in to tell him that a plane had crashed into one of the two towers of the World Trade Center. The television was turned on, and the vice president and his aides watched as another plane roared into the second tower. Cheney, who had regularly participated in "continuity of government" training drills since the early 1980s, abandoned any pretense that Bush was in charge. Seated in front of a bank of computers and television screens in the White House's underground Presidential Emergency Operations Center, Cheney grabbed a secure phone line and told Bush not to return to Washington, sending the supposed chief executive to an air force base in Nebraska. It was the vice president who insisted that all nongovernment aircraft be grounded and that American fighter pilots be given the authority to fire on any commercial aircraft that were still in the air. Cheney, who had personally visited the underground installation in the Blue Ridge Mountains that former president Dwight Eisenhower had created as a command post in case of nuclear war, ordered House Speaker Dennis Hastert, Senate majority leader Tom Daschle, and other congressional leaders to be packed onto planes and taken out of Washington to the bunkers.

"Cheney was the dominant figure on September 11," observed James Mann, the brilliant analyst of U.S. foreign policy and policy makers who serves as senior writer-in-residence at the Center for Strategic and International Studies. Even wire service reports noted that dominance, with United Press International suggesting that it "reintroduced nagging questions about who was really in charge in the Bush White House." Those questions grew louder after Cheney delivered a minute-by-minute account of the actions he took to secure the nation during an appearance the Sunday after the attacks on NBC's *Meet the Press.*

Presidential historian Douglas Brinkley summed up the point of that appearance in an interview with UPI: "It was Cheney telling the world, 'Don't worry about Shrub, I know what's going on.'" But Cheney knew his place. After he delivered that message to those American and international observers who were savvy enough to be looking for the signal, Cheney returned to the backseat. He did not make another formal television appearance for months. Working from the "secure, undisclosed location" that would become the fodder for jokes by late night comedians, the vice president who briefly revealed that he was in charge returned himself to the shadows. Cheney had no qualms about relinquishing the limelight he had briefly grabbed. There was serious work to be done now. Dick Cheney had a country to run. And he was thinking that the time had finally come for a new kind of war.

CHAPTER 1

DRESSED UP LIKE A COWBOY

Here is your country. Cherish these natural wonders, cherish the natural resources, cherish the history and romance as a sacred heritage, for your children and your children's children. Do not let selfish men or greedy interests skin your country of its beauty, its riches, or its romance.

—President Theodore Roosevelt, 1903
reflecting on Wyoming

There is such an enormous demand for gas out there around the country. Prices are high, and we need to develop those resources from the standpoint of our national energy requirements.

—Vice President Richard Cheney, 2004,
reflecting on Wyoming

Dick Cheney needed to talk to some working fellas. Four months into the new Bush-Cheney administration, the vice president had a scheme. He had been meeting in secret with the CEOs of the world's largest gas, oil, and nuclear power conglomerates, and they had cobbled together a national "energy policy" that proposed to open the Arctic National Wildlife Refuge for oil drilling, build 1,900 new power plants, and lay eighteen thou-

This cowboy is all hat: Dick Cheney likes to portray himself as a true son of Wyoming, but he was born and bred in Lincoln, Nebraska, and since college, his primary residences have been in Washington and Dallas. Cheney maintains the cowboy image by calling a $2.9 million vacation villa in a gated community in Teton County—a county with one of the highest per-capita incomes in the nation—his "home." (2003)

sand miles of fuel pipelines across what remained of the American wilderness. Oil drilling, power plant operation, and pipeline construction might wreck an already fragile environment, but these sorts of projects create jobs—at least in the short term. Unions like new jobs, Cheney reasoned, so why not get some union leaders together and talk them into backing the administration's plan to sacrifice the environment and capitalize on the energy crunch? If he could get the unions on board, Cheney figured, he could cause a heap of trouble for Democrats who might oppose his "energy plan" on environmental grounds. And he might even secure some labor support for the Republicans in future elections. But why would the leaders of the Teamsters, Steelworkers, Plumbers, Carpenters, Laborers, Steamfitters, and Seafarers jump into bed with what was already shaping up as the most rigorously antiunion administration since William McKinley lined the White House up on the side of the industrial robber barons of the late nineteenth century? Cheney thought he could counter the skepticism by reaching into his conveniently malleable past and plucking out a snippet of solidarity.

When the leaders of the twenty-three international unions—most of them from the AFL-CIO's Building and Construction Trades Department—were ushered into a secret meeting with Bush administration insiders on May 14, 2001, White House political czar Karl Rove explained to the group that they would be addressed by a fellow laboring man: Dick Cheney. After he flunked out of Yale, Cheney found brief employment as a ground man on a crew laying power lines out of Rock Springs, Wyoming. Thus, for a few months in the early 1960s, the future CEO of Halliburton carried the card of the International Brotherhood of Electrical Workers. There is no evidence to suggest that Cheney was a good union man, or even that the heavy-drinking college flunk-out was conscious of his brief residence in the house of labor. Yet, as he has throughout his long career in Washington, Cheney reached back to his brief time in Wyoming for a reference point that might suggest he was something other than the consummate Washington insider.

The pitch to labor fell flat. The union chiefs only had to shake Cheney's soft, flabby hands to recognize that they were not meeting with a workingman. By 2004, the unions that were represented in the room that day were actively campaigning against the Bush-Cheney ticket. But this failure of the fantasy was a rare one for Cheney. More often than not, the vice president gets away with peddling a wildly mythologized version of himself. And nothing is more central to the myth than the notion that Cheney is a true son of Wyoming—the Cowboy State. Of all the lies Dick Cheney tells, this one may be the biggest whopper. Yet it has served him well, providing him not only with an appealing public persona as a rugged "westerner," but with a convenient jurisdiction from which to relaunch himself whenever the vagaries of national politics dealt him a setback.

Wyoming is a great big beautiful state that has always been rich in resources such as coal, oil, and natural gas. A Republican of a very different bent from Dick Cheney recognized more than one hundred years ago that Wyoming would forever be torn between those who sought to preserve the state's natural beauty and those who sought to enrich themselves and their friends by exploiting and exporting its natural resources. "Here is your country," then president Teddy Roosevelt declared after visiting Wyoming in 1903. "Cherish these natural wonders, cherish the natural resources, cherish the history and romance as a sacred heritage, for your children and your children's children. Do not let selfish men or greedy interests skin your country of its beauty, its riches, or its romance."

A century later, Cheney would look at the same state and tell the *Denver Post,* "There is such an enormous demand for gas out there around the country. Prices are high, and we need to develop those resources from the standpoint of our national energy requirements." That's about as poetic as Cheney gets about his so-called home.

Wyoming, where a rock formation above an oil field gave its name to the Teapot Dome scandal that shocked the nation's capital in the 1920s, has a long history of being exploited by eastern politicians and Texas oilmen. With Cheney, whose primary residences since college days have been Washington and Dallas, both forms of exploitation are embodied by a single man. In this instance, however, Cheney is not exploiting just Wyoming, he is exploiting the tendency of Americans to place their faith in a "straight-shooting westerner." Americans like cowboys. But this cowboy is all hat.

The ties that bind Dick Cheney to Wyoming are far thinner than those linking Connecticut-born, eastern prep school–educated George Bush to the state of Texas. There is no Cheney ranch outside of Laramie or up the road a piece from Gillette. You won't find a weather-beaten homestead where Dick Cheney's great-grandparents spent that first rough winter on the Wyoming frontier.

The Cheney family tree has no roots in Wyoming. Descended from Pilgrim- and Puritan-era British immigrants who arrived in New England with the name "Cheyney," Dick Cheney's forebears made a not particularly romantic westward migration to Lincoln, Nebraska, where they worked as bank cashiers and government bureaucrats. The oldest of three children, Dick was born and raised in Lincoln and lived there until he was a teenager. His parents were staunch Democrats. Passionate New Dealers, Richard and Margorie Cheney cheered on the re-election of Franklin Delano Roosevelt in November 1940.

Less than three months later, they were delighted by the fact that their son Richard Bruce Cheney was born on Roosevelt's fifty-ninth birthday, January 30, 1941. Cheney would abandon the politics of his parents at an early age, embracing the conservative dogmas of the thirty-second president's bitterest foes. Dismantling the New Deal, particularly as it regulated predatory businesses that exploited states such as Wyoming, became one of his prime missions as a public figure. And while the parents loved the son, they never quite adjusted to his politics—when Cheney returned to Wyoming to run for Congress, the father would remind the son that "you can't take my vote for granted."

When he speaks at Republican fund-raising events, the vice president likes to recall that it was a Republican president, Dwight D. Eisenhower, who moved his family to Wyoming.

Like his son, Richard Herbert Cheney was a career federal bureaucrat. Unlike his son, the elder Cheney actually tried to make the bureaucracy work for someone other than himself. Employed by the U.S. Department of Agriculture with the federal Soil Conservation Service, the father was a front-line soldier in one of the great armies of the New Deal. Established during the Depression to battle soil erosion that resulted from misuse of the land, the employees of the Soil Conservation Service followed the visionary lead of founder Hugh Hammond Bennett, who preached that "no man should have the right, legally or otherwise, to recklessly or willfully destroy or unnecessarily waste any resources on which public welfare is dependent." During the presidencies of Franklin Roosevelt and Harry Truman, the conservation ethic was not just preached, but practiced.

When Eisenhower took office in 1953 as the first Republican president in two decades, however, a slow dismantling of the New Deal began, starting with the Department of Agriculture. As part of the reorganization of the agency, Cheney's father was moved west to Wyoming. "If it hadn't been for the great Republican victory in 1952," Cheney says, he might never have set foot in Wyoming.

The Cheney family decamped to Casper, a central Wyoming city that hugged the southern bank of the North Platte River. Casper owed its status as Wyoming's second largest city, and its boom-and-bust economy, to the same commodity that would fuel Dick Cheney's political and private career: oil. Just west of Casper, in 1851, Jim Bridger and Kit Carson discovered an oil spring at Poison Spider Creek. It wasn't long before the first oil well was dug near Casper, and before the nineteenth century was done, refineries began to spring up.

When oil production peaked in the 1920s, Casper's Standard Oil Refinery was the largest on earth. By the 1950s, as new techniques for extracting oil were discovered, Casper was experiencing another of its many oil booms. Thus, the Cheney family settled into a prosperous town where old west rowdiness, characterized by illegal gambling and prostitution in Casper's Sandbar district, was giving way to new west suburbanization and conservatism. Dick Cheney had a classic 1950s upbringing in Casper, although it is difficult to distinguish anything distinctly "Wyoming" about it.

The young Dick fit comfortably into the Pleasantville that Casper was becoming. Arriving in time to join the freshman class at Casper's Natrona County High School, he was the new kid determined to fit in. Dick attended Boy Scout meetings, landed an after-school job cleaning up a local variety store, wore a crew cut, and joined the Natrona Mustangs baseball and football teams. He was not all that big or strong, but, hinting at things to come, he showed up early, stayed late, and made himself the essential player on a team of better athletes. Someone else could be the star quarterback; Dick, a linebacker, managed things as the team's "co-captain." He held the equally undistinguished job of student body vice president. And, of course, he was the boyfriend of Lynne Anne Vincent. As best as anyone can remember, the first serious politicking in which Dick engaged was a popularity contest campaign to get Lynne elected as the school's Mustang Queen. "He put up a lot of posters, making sure everyone knew Lynne was the person who should be homecoming queen because of everything she does for the school," recalled Larry Stubson, a classmate. "That's the one time I remember him pushing stuff." Lynne won the queen contest, as she did most others. Lynne was always the more flamboyant partner, and as he would with presidents in the future, Dick happily managed the enterprises of a more appealing partner from behind the scenes. Lynne's claim to fame in her high school days was a baton-twirling act so spectacular that she beat out girls from across Wyoming to become state champion. Lynne twirled her way to the top using pyrotechnics. She lit both ends of her baton on fire, tossed it in the air, then caught and twirled it some more. The crowds went wild, but before Lynne could take her bow, she had to pass off the flaming baton before things got out of control.

That's where Dick came in. At the side of the stage, ever ready with a coffee can full of water, he would douse the flames—essential, but unnoticed. As Lynne, who later married the guy, told *Time* magazine after Cheney became George Bush's essential, but unnoticed second in command: "If you look back over his whole career, it's been preparation for this."

The preparation was not always as smooth as Cheney's official résumés would have Americans believe, however. Like Bill Clinton, Dick Cheney participated in Boys State, a mock political program where high schoolers ran their own state government. And, like Clinton, who excelled in the Arkansas version, Cheney took to the junior league political intriguing in Wyoming well enough to earn a ticket to Washington, D.C., for Boys Nation exercises. Such activities marked the young Dick as an up-and-comer in the eyes of a local oilman named Tom Stroock, a 1948 Yale University graduate who was always on the lookout for talented young men he could ship east. After Dick graduated from high school, Stroock arranged for Cheney's admission to Yale with a full scholarship in the fall of 1959. Unlike Joe Lieberman, who arrived on campus a year later, John Kerry, who arrived three years later, or George W. Bush, who arrived five years after him, Cheney couldn't cut it at Yale. "He didn't dig in and study like the rest of us. He probably acted the same way he did back at Casper," recalled Jacob Plotkin, who roomed with Cheney in Yale's Wright Hall when the pair were freshmen. Plotkin told the *Yale Daily News,* "Things came easily to him. He felt pretty confident. But he ran into things that he couldn't handle that way."

Like the notion of cracking a book. "Dick wasn't big on studying," explains Plotkin. A member of the freshman football team, Cheney was far more interested in playing cards with his teammates, drinking with the "Bend Your Elbow Club," and hoarding balloons for the school's end-of-the-year water balloon fight. Cheney, an A student in high school, could not make the grade at Yale. The only class that anyone recalls interesting him was an Introduction to U.S. International Relations course taught by Dr. H. Bradford Westerfield. Westerfield, who would become an internationally renowned expert on the covert operations of the Central Intelligence Agency, was a popular young professor who at the time was a fervent hawk when it came to foreign affairs. A defender of American engagement in cold war struggles, he recalls teaching his students that "the spread of Communism was being held at bay by valiant cold warriors."

Westerfield told the *Washington Post* years later that he stressed that the world was in the midst of a long-term global struggle between American-style freedom and Soviet-style totalitarianism and that he advocated for the view that it was permissible to overthrow foreign governments if the regime changes tipped the balance toward the West and against the Soviet Union.

Jacob Plotkin recalls that in a distinct departure from his response to most courses, Cheney was excited by Westerfield's class and the issues it raised. And the excitement never faded. More than forty years later, as the United States was launching an unprecedented preemptive invasion with the goal of forcing "regime change" on Iraq, Cheney continued to credit Westerfield for fostering his interest in public affairs.

Aside from those references to Westerfield's class, however, there is no evidence to suggest that any other ideas were implanted in the future vice president's head during his time at

A Little Education Can Be a
Dangerous Thing

Most teachers delight at being remembered by their former students. But when the student is Dick Cheney, it can be embarrassing.

Consider the case of Dr. H. Bradford Westerfield.

Westerfield started hearing in the 1980s that a very right-wing Republican member of Congress was dropping his name at gatherings of Yale Clubs in the western United States. "Yale graduates join these clubs and get together in places like Wyoming and Colorado and Montana. They like to invite speakers who have ties to Yale, and apparently Dick Cheney was one of them," recalled Westerfield, the Damon Wells Professor Emeritus of International Studies and Political Science at Yale, where he taught more than ten thousand students between 1957 and 2000. "The reason people contacted me was because he was apparently mentioning my name as someone who had an influence on his thinking."

It is usually an honor for an academic to be cited as an influence upon the thinking of a powerful player on the national scene. But for Westerfield, the Cheney connection seemed a stretch. He could barely recall Cheney as a student, and they had not been in contact since the Republican representative was asked to withdraw from Yale in the early 1960s. Besides, Cheney was a hawkish proponent of American military adventurism abroad, while Westerfield had a more nuanced view of the role the United States ought to play in international affairs. But the reports from Cheney's appearances at those Yale Clubs persisted. As Cheney became ever more prominent, in Congress, then as secretary of defense, and finally as the most powerful vice president in the history of the United States, Westerfield kept hearing that Cheney was telling people about how he had been inspired by the one class he took from the professor. In a profile of Cheney published by *Time* magazine in 2002, in which the writer described the vice president's penchant for unilateral war making, one of the explanations proffered by analysts was, "During a stint at Yale, Cheney was moved by a course he took from H. Bradford Westerfield, a self-described ardent hawk who believed the U.S. should use its role as the leader of the free world to fight communism wherever it took hold."

That sounded like a plausible explanation for Cheney's worldview, which was obviously not grounded in contemporary experience or knowledge of realities on the ground in countries such as Iraq. But it was discomforting to Westerfield.

The crowded Introduction to U.S. International Relations course Cheney took with Westerfield was, according to the professor, "effectively a course about the United States in the cold war. I was at the peak of my hawkishness about the cold war, and that was the perspective from which I was teaching. Whatever he picked up from me had that flavor, which is unfortunate."

Unfortunate? How so?

"I came to understand that the hawkish view was unrealistic," says Westerfield, who, like so many Americans, was jarred into a new way of thinking by watching the country's presence in Vietnam degenerate into disaster. "I remained hawkish until late 1967, early 1968, when I began to feel the war really was unwinnable. Until then, I think I was the last hawk on campus that anyone would listen to.

"I've remained dovish ever since," says the professor, a well-regarded author of numerous books on U.S. foreign policy, including *Inside the CIA's Private World*.

Westerfield's dovishness puts him in a very different camp from that of his former student. "I do not agree with his worldview today," says the professor. "I'm not even sure I understand it. He is so at odds with what we know about the world today. Unfortunately, I think it is clear that Bush is quite dependent on him. He prefers a backroom goal, but he is obviously very influential. Even Rumsfeld and Wolfowitz I do not think have the influence that Cheney does."

Westerfield last spoke with Cheney in the mid-1990s, at a memorial service for Les Aspin, Cheney's successor as secretary of defense. Cheney greeted the professor warmly but showed no interest in serious discussion with the internationally respected academic. Does Westerfield wish that he could sit Cheney down and set his former student straight? Westerfield does not think more course work would do much good. "He's obviously incorrigible. He seems to be determined to go his own way, no matter what facts he is confronted with. It's disturbing."

What to do? As the 2004 campaign heated up, Westerfield said that he had settled "very comfortably" into the camp of those who seek to bring an end to his former student's tenure in the White House. "Yes, I really want to beat Bush and Cheney. I feel that this administration doesn't want to work in coalition with the rest of the world, they really do not want to cooperate with the world. And that is precisely the wrong approach for the United States at this point."

As an expert in such matters, Westerfield says, "There is a great deal of work that needs to be done to reestablish American credibility in the world. And the first step, I think, is to elect an administration that takes our relationships with other countries more seriously."

And just for the record, what about Dick Cheney's grades in the course that so influenced him? "His grades were not particularly good," the professor says sheepishly. Pressed, Westerfield explains, "Allowing for grade inflation, his final grade would probably be a low B." Translation: Dick Cheney passed the course that sent him on the way to guiding the affairs of state with a gentleman's C.

Yale. Cheney never did get into the habit of regularly attending classes, and he left Yale after a dismal third semester, heading back to Wyoming to lick his academic wounds. Years later, Cheney would make light of his failure at Yale, joking with a *Business Week* reporter about how "I had a lack of direction, but I had a good time." In other interviews, he would claim, "I didn't like the East." Actually, Cheney liked the East enough to keep slinking back to Yale. Refusing to accept that he was not up to the Ivy League, Cheney returned to New Haven one year after he left Yale to make another attempt at completing his sophomore year. But he failed once more, getting such bad grades that his scholarship was pulled. Dick Cheney was never going to hold that Ivy League degree, let alone become a Skull and Bones alum like Kerry or Bush. He officially withdrew from Yale on June 14, 1962, and went on a bender.

Cheney likes to recall that he spent two years in the early 1960s "building power lines" with that utility crew that worked out of Rock Springs, Wyoming. And, of course, he likes to flash his union card when it's convenient. But it was clear from the start that Cheney was an atypical lineman for the county. Though he joined the union, he never embraced the working-class consciousness that made Rock Springs and surrounding Sweetwater County the backbone of populist Democratic politics in Wyoming for most of the twentieth century. Rock Springs was not a conservative city, ideologically or behaviorally. A rough-and-tumble mining town, it was settled by immigrants from Slovenia, Hungary, Poland, Italy, and, before a nasty race riot, China. Early settlers put aside piety to name a stream that flowed through the community Killpecker Creek—a reference to the unpleasant influence its waters had on the urinary tracts of those who partook of them.

Perhaps it was not surprising that taverns offering alternatives to the unappealing water supply were numerous, and young Dick Cheney, fresh from failure at Yale, found solace in the fermented beverages dispensed by the town's many drinking establishments.

Cheney may already have been a conservative, but he imbibed liberally. And injudiciously. In November 1962, around the time of the Cuban missile crisis, Cheney was busted while cruising through Cheyenne for "operating a motor vehicle while intoxicated and drunkenness." Cheney was found guilty by a Cheyenne police judge, who ordered the twenty-one-year-old's driving privileges revoked for thirty days. In addition, Cheney forfeited the $150 bond he had posted on the night of his arrest. This run-in with the law did not appear to have any significant impact on him. Eight months after the first arrest, he was busted for drunk driving by a Rock Springs cop. After the second of what he described as his "scrapes with the law," Cheney told an interviewer years later, he was forced to "think about where I was and where I was headed. I was headed down a bad road, if I continued on that course."

Lynne Vincent, who was off at college in Colorado, agreed. According to Cheney's old mentor, Tom Stroock, Lynne "was firm that she did not want to spend the rest of her life married to a lineman." True love may forgive all things, but Lynne wasn't going to forgive Dick a blue collar. "[It] was clear Lynne wasn't going to marry a lineman for the county. I had to make something of myself if I was going to consummate the relationship, and so I went back to school at the University of Wyoming and finished up my BA and a master's there . . . ," Cheney told the *Washington Post* when he was serving as secretary of defense. Actually, Cheney wasn't quite University of Wyoming material when he left Rock Springs in January 1963. Rather, he enrolled at Casper College, a junior college in his adopted hometown, for a semester of righting his record. Conveniently, this also enabled Cheney to qualify for a draft deferment based on his student status, allowing him to begin a long career of draft evasion. After proving that he could make it in junior college, Cheney shipped off to the University of Wyoming in Laramie, where the directionless Dick of the late 1950s and early 1960s suddenly became a young man in a hurry. He married Lynne in 1964, majored in political science, and started making the connections that, in barely a decade, would turn the hard-living lineman from Rock Springs into a coolly efficient White House chief of staff. Cheney got his first political break when he was awarded an internship with the Wyoming State Senate. The pay wasn't great for a married man with kids on the way—$300 for working a forty-day session—but the relationships he nurtured were important. If Cheney was not already a Republican, the internship made him one. Even after the Lyndon Johnson landslide of 1964, the last presidential election in which Wyoming went Democratic, the state senate was dominated by Republicans. So Cheney was a Republican, and he began moving in Republican circles—forging friendships with party power brokers like Wyoming House Speaker Warren Morton, future Wyoming secretary of state Joe Meyer, and future U.S. senator Alan Simpson. Those contacts with political figures who put down genuine roots in Wyoming proved to be vital after Cheney earned his BA in political science from the University of Wyoming in 1965, collected a master's degree in the same field a year later, and then hightailed it out of Wyoming. After living in the state for barely ten years, Cheney was gone for good. But with the help of Morton, Meyer, and Simpson, he was able to "return" to the state when he needed a congressional seat or a legal residence that was not in his adopted home of Texas. Whenever trouble on the national stage sent Cheney scrambling back to the state to claim it as his home, Morton could always be counted on to write a campaign check and would tell reporters, "He's just so Wyoming. He hasn't gotten highfalutin."

That didn't stop Cheney's critics from calling him a carpetbagger when, cut off from power after Gerald Ford's defeat in the 1976 presidential election, the former White House chief of staff parachuted into Wyoming to make a successful 1978 race for an open U.S. House seat. The campaign manager of one of his opponents got it right when he said, "Wyoming has always been Dick Cheney's second choice." But with Morton, Meyer, and others vouching for him, Cheney won the seat—along with a ticket back to Washington, where he took a seat on the House Interior Committee and proceeded to become one of the loudest advocates in the Congress for mining, drilling, dumping upon, and otherwise despoiling Wyoming. To this day, Cheney remains one of the nation's most ardent advocates for the view that states like Wyoming are little more than fuel sources for the kinds of places where Cheney and people like him actually live, as his vice presidential focus on energy issues has well illustrated.

After he quit the House in 1989 to serve as George Herbert Walker Bush's secretary of defense, Cheney displayed no interest in returning to Wyoming. He set up housekeeping in suburban Washington and, after a failed foray into presidential politics, moved to Dallas, Texas, to become CEO of Halliburton Co. By the late nineties, Lynne Cheney was dropping notes to her Colorado College alumni association explaining that she and Dick lived in Dallas but did "try" to get back to Wyoming now and again. The Cheneys lived in Highland Park, a tony Dallas County suburb, where Cheney registered to vote in December 1995. Like a lot of CEOs, Cheney tended to "participate" in politics by writing campaign contribution checks rather than actually voting; during his time at Halliburton, Cheney gave more than $55,000 in campaign contributions, according to the Center for Responsive Politics, but he skipped fourteen of sixteen local, state, and federal elections between 1995 and 2000—Cheney did, however, cast a ballot in the 1996 presidential race and the 1998 Texas gubernatorial race, when, presumably, he voted for fellow Texan George W. Bush. While Cheney was not exactly a good citizen of Texas, he was clearly a resident of the state— where he held a driver's license listing his Highland Park address, registered his vehicles, and paid his taxes.

That became a problem when, in the summer of 2000, Cheney selected himself to serve as George W. Bush's running mate. The Twelfth Amendment to the U.S. Constitution prohibits the president and the vice president from living in the same state. So, according to the highest law of the land, Texan Dick Cheney was not qualified to run with Texan George Bush. What to do? Cheney quickly "went Wyoming" once more, declaring himself to be a resident of a state where he did not live. In November, Cheney voted for himself and Bush on a Wyoming ballot, before moving to the vice presidential residence in Washington.

But there remained the inconvenient question of where in Wyoming this faux westerner would make his official "residence." Suffice it to say that the most powerful man in the world was not going back to the blue-collar towns of Casper or Rock Springs. Rather, Cheney declared an elegant $2.9 million vacation villa in Teton County to be "home." A playground of the rich and famous, Teton County has frequently had the highest per capita income in the nation.

Home to Jackson Hole and other ski resort towns, the county attracts out-of-state elites with names such as DuPont and Rockefeller. Housing values are so high that the international auction houses Sotheby's and Christie's are among the local Realtors in the county, where the running joke is that the billionaires are pricing the millionaires out of town. In Jackson, according to writer Don Pitcher, "The cowboy hats all look as if the price tags just came off. This sure isn't Rock Springs!" Explains Pitcher, "In other parts of Wyoming, Jackson is viewed with a mixture of awe and disdain—awe over its booming economy, disdain that Jackson is not a 'real' town, just a false front put up to sell things to outsiders." The king of the outsiders is Dick Cheney, who flies into Jackson Hole Airport, where an infusion of federal funds has expanded a small runway that now accommodates Air Force Two, and is whisked off in a motorcade of black Suburbans with dark-tinted windows to Jackson Hole's only gated community.

On the "money" side of the gate is "a complex dominated by an "enormous main building [that] looks like a beautifully decorated airport, with a beautifully decorated restaurant overlooking beautifully decorated condominiums," according to author and Jackson Hole native Nathaniel Burt, who explains, "You could fly in from L.A., play golf, fly out and never know you'd left home." Dick Cheney's Wyoming is, according to Burt, "an extreme manifestation of the new Jackson Hole of far-flung millionaires and billionaires from all over who have built massive mansions and swimming pools so they can enjoy the simple life of the Old West."

Behind the gate that keeps the real Wyoming at bay, Dick Cheney has found a corner of the state that he appreciates as much as another Republican, Teddy Roosevelt, appreciated the Wyoming wilderness that Cheney's "open for business" energy policies are rapidly destroying. It is here, in a haven of the super-rich that happens to be located in Wyoming, that an oil industry CEO, or even a vice president, can relax after a day of despoiling the environment, clip the tag off a new hat, pull on some shiny boots, and dress up like a cowboy.

Family values?: Precisely nine months and two days after the Selective Service eliminated constraints on drafting childless married men during the Vietnam War, Dick Cheney's first child, Elizabeth, was born. Despite the fact that daughter Mary grew up to be a lesbian liaison for the GOP, Cheney declared his support for a constitutional amendment barring marriage for lesbians and gays, and wife Lynne suppressed the republication of a racy romance novel featuring lesbian love that she wrote in 1981. (1978)

CHAPTER 2

DEFERRED PATRIOTISM

I had other priorities in the sixties than military service.
—Dick Cheney, 1989, explaining why he dodged
the draft during the Vietnam War

*In my mind there is no doubt that because he had
"other priorities" someone died or was injured in his
place.*
—Former secretary of veterans affairs Jesse Brown,
2000, referring to Dick Cheney

When Dick Cheney arrived on the University of Wisconsin (UW) campus in the fall of 1966, it was his stated goal to become a specialist in politics, public policy, and the ways of government. For a still reasonably young man with such interests, it would seem that the fates had been generous. He had come to precisely the right place at precisely the right moment to join the passionate and public foreign policy debate of his lifetime. The Madison campus, where one of the more enlightened faculties in the nation taught one of the more politically engaged and energized student bodies in history, was an internationally recognized center of the student activism that would define the late 1960s. But Cheney, a graduate student whose announced plan was to become a professor of political science, did not join the burgeoning dialogue about the propriety of the war in Vietnam in particular and the cold war in general. Rather, he grumbled that it was "a distraction."

Dick Cheney came to Madison as the last man of the 1950s, determined that his political engagements would involve carefully calculated career moves designed to take him ever closer to power, not the matters of the heart that they were for student activists like Paul Soglin, a campus radical who would become the "boy mayor" of Madison at about the same time Cheney was slinking out of the Nixon White House to avoid association with the Watergate scandal. "Dick Cheney may have gone to college in the sixties. But there was nothing 'sixties' about him," explains Soglin. "There were always these guys who saw everything that was going on then as an annoyance, something that got in the way of their personal agenda. Cheney was one of them."

Cheney didn't go in for street activism, liberal or conservative. While most students at UW cast their lot with the Left, a brave band of conservatives that included future Bush administration secretary of health and human services Tommy Thompson pulled together a Young Americans for Freedom chapter and protested the protesters. Cheney did not join either team. As at Yale, where he showed absolutely no interest in the town-and-gown civil rights organizing by some of the more liberal students—or in the criticism of that activism by the conservative *Yale Daily News*—Cheney maintained his distance from democracy's messier manifestations.

"I was on campus during the years when Cheney was, but I don't remember him. No one I know remembers him," says Ed Garvey, a Madison lawyer and former Democratic nominee for governor of Wisconsin who studied at UW Law School when

Cheney was doing graduate work in political science on campus. "At this incredible time in our history, Cheney was a no-show."

Pulitzer Prize–winning author David Maraniss, who interviewed the vice president for his book *They Marched into Sunlight,* says Cheney just couldn't be bothered. "I think he's emblematic of a certain type. He wasn't against the war, just didn't want anything to do with it," explains Maraniss. "He wanted to get on with his life and not let the world get in the way."

Unfortunately, the world got in the way of a lot of young men who, like Cheney, were of draft age when the U.S. troop presence in Vietnam began to rise in the mid-1960s. As a result, there was one sense in which Cheney mirrored the actions, if not the politics, of his fellow students. Dick Cheney was definitely opposed to the draft, at least as far as it affected him.

In an era when many young men avoided military service for many reasons, few were so meticulous about the endeavor as Dick Cheney. Indeed, when the future secretary of defense arrived on the University of Wisconsin campus, he was arguably one of the most accomplished—and inventive—draft dodgers in the country. Unlike George W. Bush, who performed some sort of service—ill defined and unrecorded as it may have been—in the Texas Air National Guard, Dick Cheney reacted to the prospect of wearing his country's uniform as a man with a deadly allergy to olive drab. Between 1963 and 1965, Cheney used his student status at Casper College and the University of Wyoming to apply for and receive four 2S draft deferments. As the fight in Vietnam heated up, Cheney fought like a true warrior to defend his deferments. Twenty-two days after Congress approved the Gulf of Tonkin Resolution in August 1964, raising the prospect of a rapid expansion of the draft, Dick "conveniently"—in the words of a 1991 *Washington Post* profile—married Lynne. Even if his student deferment was lifted, his status as a married man might have made the draft board more sensitive to Cheney's consistent, if frequently reframed, argument that he was needed on the home front. But the Vietnamese were not cooperating with Cheney's plan.

The war kept demanding more and more young American men, and the range of those who were eligible for the draft expanded rapidly. On May 19, 1965, it looked as if Dick Cheney's deferments would no longer protect him. He was reclassified with the most dangerous draft status: 1A, "available for military service." No longer protected by his eternal student status, Cheney was still counting on his marriage to keep him off the front lines. But events were conspiring against him.

Struggling to maintain the manpower for a war that he still thought could be won, President Lyndon Johnson announced on July 28, 1965, that draft call-ups would double. Three months later, on October 26, 1965, the Selective Service constraints on the drafting of childless married men were lifted. Da Nang was calling. And it did not look as though Dick had any excuses left. But there was one way for ambitious young men to avoid serving their country while maintaining their political viability. If Cheney had a child, he would be reclassified 3A, the status that allowed married men with dependents to remain out of uniform. That would work. Except, of course, that Cheney did not have a child—yet. Precisely nine months and two days after the Selective Service eliminated special protections for childless married men, Cheney was no longer childless. His daughter Elizabeth was born on July 28, 1966. Convenient? Coincidence? That's not Cheney's style. Writer Timothy Noah did the math and suggested that the timing of Elizabeth's arrival "would seem to indicate that the Cheneys, though doubtless planning to have children sometime, were seized with an untamable passion the moment Dick Cheney became vulnerable to the draft. And acted on it. Carpe diem! Who says government policy can't affect human behavior."

Of course, Dick Cheney left nothing to chance. He applied for 3A status immediately, receiving it on January 19, 1966, when Lynne was still in the first trimester of her pregnancy.

Twenty-three years later, when Cheney appeared before the Senate to plead the case for his confirmation as George Herbert Walker Bush's secretary of defense, the nominee was questioned about his failure to serve. Cheney responded by saying that he "would have obviously been happy to serve had I been called."

In a more truthful moment that same year, Cheney admitted to *Washington Post* reporter George C. Wilson that "I had other priorities in the sixties than military service." Cheney's lie to the Senate has never caused much concern, but that "other priorities" line has dogged him. After Cheney selected himself to serve on the 2000 Republican ticket, former secretary of veterans affairs Jesse Brown, a Vietnam veteran who was disabled by a gunshot wound to his right arm, said, "As a former marine who was wounded and nearly lost his life, I personally resent that comment. I resent that he had 'other priorities,' when fifty-eight thousand people died and over three hundred thousand returned wounded and disabled. In my mind there is no doubt that because he had 'other priorities' someone died or was injured in his place." That's a rough assessment, but it is true that at least a dozen men from Cheney's adopted hometown of Casper, Wyoming—aged nineteen to forty-seven—died in Vietnam during the period when Cheney might have served.

Because local draft boards had to fill quotas, when a man who was eligible to serve got a deferment, someone else had to fill the slot. The vagaries of draft quotas, military service, and the war itself make it impossible to say whether Leroy Robert Cardenas or Walter Elmer Handy or Douglas Tyrone Patrick or any of the other sons of Casper who died in Southeast Asia might have survived the war years and gone on to explore their "other priorities" had Dick Cheney responded to his country's call. But that doesn't stop some of those who served from asking, "Who died in your place, Dick Cheney?" That's a question Vietnam veteran Dennis Mansker raises on his Web site, where he maintains a list of the dead from Casper. Maybe Cheney did have other priorities, Mansker argues above the list, but "so did these guys."

What exactly were Cheney's other priorities? As Secretary Brown says, "Too many people died during that period of time . . . for us not to ask those hard questions." As best anyone can tell, Cheney's chief priority, as it has been ever since, was getting Dick Cheney as close to power as possible. Thus, though he came to Madison in pursuit of a doctorate, Cheney didn't exactly dive into academia. Indeed, after he nominated himself for vice president, the University of Wisconsin communications office issued one of the more painful "he's one of ours (sort of)" press releases ever produced. Under the headline CHENEY HAS STRONG UW TIES, it was revealed that George W. Bush's ticket partner "was a full-time student for his first three semesters and a part-time student for the final semester." That would seem to suggest that Cheney, working within some sort of time frame toward some sort of goal, was busy completing the requirements of the PhD program in which he was enrolled. He wasn't. Cheney says now that he "did all the work for my doctorate except the dissertation." Anyone who has gone through life with ABD (all but dissertation) after their name for any amount of time will tell you that's a pretty big "except." Of course, the truth is that Cheney's commitment to his graduate studies at the University of Wisconsin ran only a tiny bit deeper than his commitment to his undergraduate studies. The long-suffering folks in the UW communications office came up with only one political science professor who could remember Cheney, M. Crawford Young, who said, "He was a quiet and competent member of my class." Talk about a recommendation!

So if Cheney wasn't a big man on campus, what was he? An intern. When it came to finessing his way onto the staffs of powerful political figures, Cheney was a regular Monica Lewinsky. Throughout his time at UW, the future vice president was a gofer for Republican politicians. He started out by securing a National Center for Education in Politics internship in the office of Wisconsin governor Warren Knowles, one of the last of the great midwestern moderate Republicans. A dapper career politician who was groomed at one point as a prospective running mate for Richard Nixon, Knowles surrounded himself with bright young men who would go on to become dominant players in the business and political life of Wisconsin. Among the best and brightest crowd that surrounded Knowles, Cheney was anything but a star. But, as would prove to be the case throughout his public career, Cheney had no shame in the pursuit of power; he would do any job that got him close to the right people. And in the Knowles administration that job was holding the button bag. When Knowles traveled around the state, Cheney was sent along to follow the governor around, carrying a bag of lapel badges inscribed with the slogan "We Like It Here." Cheney recalled years later that it was his responsibility to "make sure I got a button on everybody." It was a long way from controlling the fate of the planet as the most powerful vice president in history, but holding the button bag was a start. And it put Cheney in the right place at the right time.

In 1966, one of the brightest young Republicans in the country, a wealthy and handsome state representative named Bill Steiger, beat the Democratic congressman who represented east-central Wisconsin. Steiger headed off to Washington with big ambitions for himself and for his party. A favorite of the liberal Ripon Society, Steiger was the sort of Republican who toured the South in the early 1960s, condemning segregationist Democrats and urging young whites and African Americans to join Lincoln's Grand Old Party in the cause of civil rights. Though he came to Washington as part of a large class of new Republican representatives that included George Herbert Walker Bush and other rising stars in the party, Steiger was determined to make his mark not just as someone grasping for the next rung on the political ladder, but as a serious policy maker. Recognizing that he needed to build an effective staff, Steiger sent word to Knowles that he was looking for bright young aides to join him in Washington. Cheney, who had qualified for an American Political Science Association fellowship to work on Capitol Hill, needed a congressional sponsor, and though they did not necessarily see eye to eye on the issues, Steiger would do nicely.

Unfortunately for Cheney, Governor Knowles and his aides were not sure that they wanted to recommend the aging student who carried the button bag. A Knowles staffer recalls, "We got the word from Steiger that he was looking for someone to come out and help on policy stuff in his office. We all liked Steiger, so there was a discussion about who would go. Then, when it got serious, people started begging off—one guy wanted to go to law school, someone else had already started a family, someone else was interested in getting into business in Wisconsin. Finally, it came down to Dick. I think he was the fourth choice. Of course, he wanted it. He wanted to get to Washington in the worst way." So it was, in early 1968, that Cheney ended his formal education and made his first great grab for power.

Seven years earlier, Dick Cheney was a Yale reject with a drinking problem and slim prospects. Seven years hence, he would be the White House chief of staff. By avoiding an inconvenient detour to Vietnam, Cheney had made the most of the 1960s. While other young men fought his country's battles, in the rice paddies of Southeast Asia and in the streets of American cities where the civil rights and antiwar movements challenged corrupt orthodoxies, Dick Cheney pursued his "other priorities." In so doing, he began the meticulous accumulation of power that would, eventually, enable him to send young men and women to die in distant wars every bit as unnecessary and misguided as the Vietnam conflict, while at home he restored the old order that the more idealistic members of his generation believed had been banished.

Our gang: Beginning with the Nixon administration, the alliance of Donald Rumsfeld and Dick Cheney was a classic Washington coupling, with Rumsfeld out front and Cheney covering his back. After Nixon's fall, Cheney followed Rumsfeld as Gerald Ford's chief of staff. (1975)

CHAPTER 3

DICK RISING

Jerry Ford gave me an opportunity at thirty-four to run the White House.

—Dick Cheney, 2003

Whenever his private ideology was exposed, he appeared somewhat to the right of Ford, Rumsfeld, or, for that matter, Genghis Khan.

—Ford aide Robert Hartmann, 1980, describing Cheney

White House Chief of Staff Richard Cheney . . . is blamed by Ford insiders for a succession of campaign blunders.

—Evans and Novak, 1976

Dick Cheney arrived in Washington as a man long on ambition and short on accomplishment. He was twenty-seven years old, with a wife and a child and a couple of degrees from the University of Wyoming. Yet while other men his age were already well on their way to establishing themselves as political players, he had come to the capital as a glorified intern. Cheney was going to need to grab hold of someone else's coattails if he hoped to move up fast—someone like Don Rumsfeld. Unlike Cheney, the rootless faux athlete, faux intellectual, faux westerner, Rumsfeld was the real thing. Born nine years before Cheney to a prosperous family, raised in the suburbs of Chicago, he had been a star wrestler at his high school and at Princeton—where he was such a master of the mats that he captained the squad and was considered for a place on the U.S. Olympic team. Rumsfeld was completely different from Cheney: he actually graduated from an Ivy League school, Princeton. Then he volunteered for the U.S. Navy, training as a fighter pilot in the thick of the cold war. By the late 1950s, he was serving as an aide to Michigan congressman Robert Griffin, one of the barons of the House and co-author of the anti-labor Landrum-Griffin Act of 1959. Before he was thirty, Rumsfeld was back in Illinois, positioning himself to win a House seat of his own, representing Chicago's wealthiest suburbs. By the late 1960s, when Cheney finally showed up in Washington, Rumsfeld was already serving his third term in the House and developing a reputation as one of the young stars of the Republican Party. He had helped to engineer a Republican caucus coup that made a relatively young Michigan representative named Gerald Ford the House minority leader, thus guaranteeing he could rise as fast and as far as was possible for a Republican member of Congress in those days of Democratic dominance. But Rumsfeld was not satisfied serving in what was then referred to as the "permanent minority." Looking to move up and out, he was cozying up to Richard Nixon, the man the party would run for president in 1968.

That was the year of Cheney's arrival in Washington. And he was attracted to Rumsfeld immediately. Cheney's attachment to Rumsfeld was so powerful that Robert Hartmann, who as an aide to President Gerald Ford observed the two men up close through much of the mid-1970s, would write in 1980, "Cheney's adult life has been devoted to the study of political science and the service of Donald Rumsfeld." The relationship did not, however, begin on a good note. Cheney tried for a job on the high-flying House member's staff in early 1968. Unfortunately, while Cheney wanted to get as close to Rumsfeld as he could, Rumsfeld was not similarly inclined. The rejection stung. Almost twenty years later, after he had experienced the crumbling of the Nixon White House, managed Gerald Ford out of office, and suffered several heart attacks, Cheney said of the brief interview with Rumsfeld, "It was one of the more unpleasant experiences of my life. . . . The truth is I flunked the interview," he explained in a 1986 speech describing his relationship with Rumsfeld. "After half an hour, it was clear to both of us that there was no possibility that I could work for him."

Cheney learned a life lesson that day: Never put yourself in a position where someone else is evaluating you. Rather, take charge of even the most picayune aspects of the evaluation process and then, when you have successfully chipped away at all the other candidates, recommend Dick Cheney. He would apply the strategy many times over the years to come, most successfully in 2000, when he was given the supposedly thankless task of evaluating prospective running mates for George W. Bush. For the time being, however, Cheney was stuck with Bill Steiger. That wasn't a particularly bad position to be in. Steiger was smart, experienced beyond his years, and very much in the circle of GOP "stars" that included Texas congressman George H. W. Bush and, of course, Don Rumsfeld. Only three years older than Cheney, Steiger had served three terms in the Wisconsin State Legislature, beaten a Democratic incumbent to win a seat in the U.S. House, and arrived in Washington with pundits already charting his path to the presidency. Moderately critical of the Vietnam War, Steiger was opposed to the draft and led the congressional fight for an all-volunteer army. He chastened conservatives within the Republican ranks, warning that they had to stop refusing to admit that urban unrest and air pollution were serious issues. "If we do that, then we're kidding ourselves about the course of the party and about honoring Abraham Lincoln here," he declared at a 1967 Lincoln Day dinner in Wisconsin.

Dick Cheney likes to say that when he worked for Steiger in 1969, he helped the congressman investigate campus radicalism. That's true, up to a point. As the youngest member of the House, Steiger did take an interest in the antiwar demonstrations that were erupting on American campuses in the late 1960s. But he was not exactly "investigating" them, as Steiger explained in an interview with the Madison *Capital Times,* a homestate newspaper. Rather, Steiger joined a handful of the most progressive members of the Republican House caucus, including Michigan's Don Riegle, who would later switch parties and serve in the Senate as a Democrat, and California's Pete McCloskey, who would mount an antiwar challenge to Nixon in the 1972 presidential primaries, in an effort to avert a crackdown by congressional conservatives and the new Nixon administration. Defending academic and intellectual freedom, Steiger and the others warned against proposals to require colleges to implement codes of conduct for campus behavior in order to receive federal funding. Steiger attended a Students for a Democratic Society meeting on the University of Wisconsin campus in May 1969 and listened to a visiting Black Panther leader from Chicago. Far from being frightened by his encounter with revolutionary politics, Steiger said, he came away with the impression that "the disaffection and alienation which one finds in student revolutionaries is widespread throughout many student bodies. Vast numbers of students are just as deeply disturbed as the so-called revolutionaries. The difference is that they have not yet rejected completely the view that they should not resort to violence." Passing repressive legislation, Steiger argued, would only increase disaffection and, ultimately, violence. "We have to sell them [students] on the idea that democracy works, that the system is responsible, that changes can be effected through legitimate channels. Students will not be coerced, they will not be cowed by the threat of punishment or the application of overwhelming force."

While Steiger recognized that the campus dissent in the late 1960s was a legitimate and important cry for the country to address critical issues, his aide came away with a different impression. Cheney, who was still technically a UW student in the spring of 1969, would tell the *New Yorker* more than three decades later that the visit he made to the UW campus with Steiger so turned him off, he decided then and there that he did not want to continue his studies and become a college professor.

Just as there is little evidence to suggest that Cheney expanded his intellectual horizons during his sojourn as a graduate student, there is even less evidence that his perspective was improved by his time on Steiger's staff. Several years ago, in a conversation with the vice president, I mentioned Steiger to him. Great man, wonderful man, great Republican," Cheney said with his usual clipped delivery. Yet it is difficult to imagine a Republican more different from the Bill Steiger of the 1960s and 1970s than the Dick Cheney of today. In fact, Steiger's agenda from those days, which emphasized environmental protection, expansion of legal services for the poor, and the need to increase regulations to protect workers from on-the-job injuries—before his death in 1978 at the age of forty, Steiger joined Democrats in the battle to pass the Occupational Safety and Health Act—sounds perilously similar to the brand of mainstream, problem-solving politics that Cheney was busy attacking in 2004 when he toured the country condemning Massachusetts senator John Kerry as a dangerous liberal. Cheney, who even in the late 1960s was already proving to be more interested in power than in principles, was never inclined toward Steiger's brand of Republicanism. He wanted to follow another Republican, Don Rumsfeld, off Capitol Hill and into the new Nixon administration.

Rumsfeld, whose first campaign had employed Jeb Stuart Magruder, Nixon's future Watergate co-conspirator, proudly wore his "Nixon's the One" pin during the 1968 campaign. He served as the campaign's eyes and ears on the ground in Chicago during the chaotic Democratic National Convention, calling in breathless reports to Tricky Dick, who delighted in the details of riots in the streets and pandemonium on the convention floor. That service to the campaign merited reward with a high-profile position in the new administration, argued Rumsfeld, who suffered from no deficit of ego or ambition. But the three-term congressman did not get the cabinet slot or the Republican National Committee chairmanship he desired. Rather, after two preferred picks turned down the job, Rumsfeld was invited to join the administration as head of the Office of Economic Opportunity (OEO), a Great Society remnant set up to coordinate War on Want initiatives in the heady days when President Lyndon Johnson declared that it was possible to "conquer poverty." Since Rumsfeld had been a frequent congressional critic of the programs that the agency administered, he was, in the perverse thinking of the new president, ideally suited to run the OEO. In a reflection on the new administration's priorities, Rumsfeld and Nixon agreed that heading the agency charged with eliminating poverty was not a particularly prestigious assignment, so the congressman was also named an "assistant to the president" and assigned an office in the White House. Dick Cheney was drooling by now. He just had to get a gig with Rumsfeld.

Official and semiofficial biographies of Cheney from this period are comic documents. *Congressional Quarterly* suggests that "Cheney's ideas about reorganizing the Office of Economic Opportunity attracted the attention of another Republican representative, Donald Rumsfeld, who was helping reorganize the Office of Economic Opportunity for the administration of Richard Nixon." Technically, that's true. But, as with so much of the story of Cheney's political rise, the devil is in the details. While the Cheney mythology makes it sound as if Rumsfeld came across a thoughtful essay by the young academic in some policy journal, the fact is that Cheney was in the habit of regularly rifling through Steiger's papers looking for "opportunities." Dave Gribben, one of Cheney's oldest friends, revealed those details in a 2001 interview with journalist and historian James Mann. As Mann explains it in his brilliant book *Rise of the Vulcans: The History of Bush's War Cabinet,* Cheney was working in Steiger's office in the spring of 1969 "when he noticed a note on Steiger's desk from Rumsfeld, looking for advice and help in his new OEO job. Cheney spotted an opportunity. Over a weekend he wrote an unsolicited memo for Steiger on how to staff and run a federal agency. The following week Steiger passed on the memo to Rumsfeld. A few weeks after reading it, Rumsfeld called up Cheney and offered him a position as his special assistant."

For the next thirty years, Cheney would be Rumsfeld's aide, ally, friend, and confidant. Theirs proved to be a classic Washington insider coupling, with Rumsfeld out front and Cheney covering his back. Not until 2000, when Rumsfeld was angling for the assignment from papa Bush to serve as George W.'s minder, did Cheney finally elbow Rumsfeld aside to grab the grail that was the Republican vice presidential nomination. By then, however, both men had slogged through so many swamps together that it was impossible for Rumsfeld to challenge Cheney. In the end, every tag team has a dominant grappler. Just about anyone who knew the two men would have bet that the more openly ambitious and far more accomplished Rumsfeld would forever remain the top man. But in the final battle, it turned out that Cheney was the most cruel and calculating of the pair.

For the time being, however, there was no question that Rumsfeld was the boss. Cheney, the rejected suitor who kept coming back until Rumsfeld finally accepted him, made it his business to meet and master the most menial demands of a man who did not intend to finish his federal career as head of the Office of Economic Opportunity. As he had back in the days at Natrona County High School, where he stood off to the side of the stage waiting to douse Lynne Vincent's flaming batons, Cheney quickly made it clear that no responsibility was beneath him. In so doing, he positioned himself as a Watson to Rumsfeld's Sherlock Holmes. Perhaps not the best or the brightest member on an OEO staff that included a future secretary of defense (Frank Carlucci), a future U.S. trade representative (Mickey Cantor), a future Environmental Protection Agency chief (Christine Todd Whitman), and a future U.S. senator and presidential candidate (Bill Bradley), Cheney remained Rumsfeld's essential assistant.

Cheney's loyalty was unyielding, even when Rumsfeld

veered to the left of Cheney's ideological comfort zone. It was no secret that Nixon wanted the OEO's mission downsized—at least in part because Republican governors were griping about all the federal money that was being spent to organize the poor in their states—but Rumsfeld was not entirely enthusiastic about deconstructing his newly acquired power base. Governors like California's Ronald Reagan and Ohio's Jim Rhodes despised the OEO for providing the funding for legal services programs that helped migrant farmworkers sue the agribusiness interests that funded Republican campaigns. Yet Rumsfeld started making the case for expanded federal funding of legal aid initiatives. Rumsfeld was not exactly a flaming liberal—he set up a classically Nixonian vetting process to assure that OEO funding did not go to "revolutionaries" and "subversives." But when he told reporters that he wanted to do "justice for the poor," it became clear that he would not last long at the helm of this particular agency.

Luckily, for Rumsfeld—and by extension Cheney—Nixon thought his OEO administrator was something of a hipster. The president, who was having a hard time figuring out why so many young people were referring to him as a "war criminal," frequently consulted Rumsfeld, who wore stylish aviator glasses and longish sideburns and seemed, in Nixon's view, to be more in touch with the liberal-leaning youth than, say, Attorney General John Mitchell. A note in the diary of Nixon's chief of staff, H.R. "Bob" Haldeman, for March 21, 1970, read, "[Nixon] wants Don Rumsfeld brought more into the inner councils." Haldeman recorded his view that Rumsfeld was "slimy," but Nixon was enamored of the former congressman. "He's young, he's thirty-nine years old, he's a hell of a spokesman," the president said of Rumsfeld. So intrigued was Nixon that he and Haldeman once broke from preparations for a major speech on Vietnam to discuss Rumsfeld's presidential prospects—Rummy had "the charisma for national office," Nixon observed, but he lacked "the backbone." That said, Nixon wanted Rumsfeld around; he just didn't want the younger man giving away money to antipoverty organizers anymore. So Rumsfeld was moved out of his OEO position in early 1971 and over to the White House as a "counselor" to the president. With Rumsfeld came Cheney. Neither man was precisely clear on his assignment. Nixon aides recalled that the more overtly ambitious Rumsfeld would slip into the Oval Office to plant seeds of doubt in Nixon's head regarding Vice President Spiro Agnew, in hopes that Nixon would shuffle the crooked former governor of Maryland off the 1972 Republican ticket and look for a younger running mate like, um, Don Rumsfeld.

Cheney, for whom memories of intern days spent holding the button bag for Warren Knowles remained fresh, was not shooting so high. Officially a "staff assistant," he was looking for a position with a title that would read better on a résumé. It came in the fall of 1971, when Nixon tapped Rumsfeld to head the White House Cost of Living Council. Predictably, Rumsfeld tapped Cheney as his assistant director in charge of scut work. Cheney toiled in relative obscurity in that position, spending much of his time studying Richard Nixon as a political player. For Cheney, who had never been all that serious about his academic studies, Nixon provided a practical education about the art of acquiring power. John Dean, who served as White House counsel during the Nixon years, would observe three decades later that Cheney appeared to have been particularly influenced by Nixonian moves to make the executive branch the dominant player in the federal government.

"Nixon was ignoring Congress in four areas," recalled Dean. "First, he refused to spend money the Congress had appropriated for programs he didn't believe in, simply impounding the money. Second, he ignored Congress's efforts to get him to cut back or end the war in Vietnam, often increasing and widening the war when they were in recess. Third, he regularly invoked executive privilege, thus denying Congress information it sought as aid in its job of conducting oversight of the executive branch. Fourth, finally, and in what was probably his most offensive act of the four, Nixon implemented a total reorganization of the executive branch by executive order. The result was to give Congress no say over departments and agencies that had years earlier been created by Congress."

Sound familiar? It did to Dean when Cheney began ranting in 2002—during a struggle to block Congress from obtaining information regarding the work of his energy task force—about how, "in thirty-four years, I have repeatedly seen an erosion of the powers and ability of the president of the United States to do his job." Dean explained, "His reference to 'thirty-four years' is quite clear. About thirty-four years ago, in 1969, Dick Cheney joined the Nixon administration. . . . Cheney's reference to the erosion of presidential powers thus appears to relate to the Nixon presidency and Watergate." Dean continued, "After Watergate, Congress moved from its lowest point back to a more normal posture vis-à-vis the executive branch. These laws [a reference to legislation passed by Congress to restore the traditional balance of powers] represent the 'erosion' of presidential powers that Cheney has witnessed from both ends of Pennsylvania Avenue.

In truth, they are more accurately described as a restoration of power previously stolen by Nixon from Congress." Three decades after assistant director Dick Cheney left the Nixon White House, Dean argued, Vice President Dick Cheney was busy trying to return to a state of affairs he knew and loved, that of the pre-Watergate Nixon White House.

It is important to note that for all of his passion for power and secrecy, Cheney was never enough of a player in the Nixon White House to become a "plumber," as the Watergate conspirators came to be known. Watergate plots and cover-ups were above Cheney's pay grade. He was in the Nixon administration as a Rumsfeld man, not in his own right. And as readers will recall, Haldeman thought Rumsfeld was "slimy." Rumsfeld was not on the "enemies list," but there was no question that Haldeman and a number of other key players in the administration wanted the troublingly "liberal" Illinoisan—who had begun to make dovish noises regarding the Vietnam War—out of the White House in the worst way. Conveniently, Rumsfeld wanted a more prestigious position, preferably something that would allow him to beef up his foreign policy credentials. Everything came together nicely after Nixon won reelection by a landslide in 1972 and, in short order, made Rumsfeld ambassador to the North Atlantic Treaty Organization. Thus, as White House aides were committing high crimes and misdemeanors left and right, Rumsfeld was being wined and dined in Paris and Brussels. Unfortunately for Cheney, Rumsfeld did not have room in his suitcase for an assistant whose foreign policy "experience" consisted of a couple of classes in college and graduate school. Fortunately for Cheney, Rumsfeld's exit meant the younger man would leave the Nixon White House at precisely the point when smart rats were jumping ship. Cheney was too unproven and, frankly, too unimpressive to be handed a position of authority. So he was nudged out of the White House just as Watergate was evolving from an irritation into a crisis. As the Nixon presidency crumbled, Cheney was working in complete obscurity with Bradley, Woods & Company, a Washington firm that advised investment banks. But he would not be outside the White House for long. Soon, Dick Cheney would be calling the shots.

When it became clear that the Watergate scandal was indeed, as Dean described it, "a cancer on the presidency," responsible Republicans began to put distance between themselves and Nixon. In May 1973, for instance, Cheney's old boss, Bill Steiger, declared himself to be "appalled by the spectacle of illegal acts, the concealments and other attempts to circumvent laws." But the Rumsfeld-Cheney axis adopted a more cynical approach. They avoided public discussion of the scandal—knowing that Nixon's radar was always on, searching for the slightest slight—while privately seeking to buck up the president's spirits. In his 1978 memoir, *RN,* the thirty-seventh president recalled how, as the impeachment process was gearing up, Rumsfeld offered to return home as a foot soldier in the battle to save the Nixon presidency. Nixon did not take Rumsfeld up on his offer. That decision set the course for the next thirty years of American history. By leaving his NATO ambassador at a safe distance from the ugly struggle that would destroy the ambitions of so many men, Nixon made it possible for Rumsfeld and Cheney to become essential players in succeeding Republican administrations, beginning with that of Gerald Ford.

When Agnew was forced to resign the vice presidency in 1973, in a "throw the excess weight off the sinking ship" move,

Nixon became the first president in American history to select a new vice president during the course of his term. Nixon wanted someone who was free of scandal, yet at the same time unthreatening. Rumsfeld did his best to float his name as a replacement, but that was not to be. He did, however, get the next best thing when Nixon selected Ford, Rumsfeld's old congressional colleague. A man of Congress, with genuinely moderate instincts, Ford would assume the presidency in August 1974 in the midst of the most serious constitutional crisis in American history. It might not have been the perfect way to enter the Oval Office, but there were some advantages to succeeding a scandal-plagued president. Because so many Nixon aides had been imprisoned, indicted, and otherwise shamed, Ford was reasonably free to pick his own team. Ford started by tapping Rumsfeld, who in turn tapped Cheney. On the day before Nixon's resignation, Ford called Rumsfeld at NATO headquarters in Brussels and asked the ambassador to come home and serve on the transition team. When Rumsfeld flew into Dulles International Airport, Cheney was waiting. Cheney was exactly where he wanted to be: at Rumsfeld's side and in charge of evaluating others—in this case, the men and women who would make up Ford's domestic policy team. Rumsfeld and Cheney started by making themselves, respectively, Ford's White House chief of staff and deputy chief of staff.

Rumsfeld and Cheney were, in the view of historian James Mann, "a complementary pair, each offering traits the other didn't possess. Rumsfeld was full of energy; Cheney was low-keyed. Rumsfeld was overflowing with words and ideas; Cheney, the laconic westerner, never used a word beyond what the situation required. Rumsfeld always seemed to want more: more turf, expanded missions, a bigger job; Cheney appeared to the world as unfailingly modest and patient." Of course, as Rumsfeld would learn when Cheney eventually elbowed him out of the vice presidency, the younger man's patience was that of a viper waiting to strike. But in 1974 and 1975, Rumsfeld and Cheney were preparing to strike others, not each other. Well aware that Ford was weak and that individuals other than the president would control this White House, they set out to ensure that they and their allies would end up in charge—much as they would later combine to take charge of George W. Bush's White House. A number of people stood in the way of their schemes, however, including Robert Hartmann, a former newspaper reporter who had served on Ford's congressional and vice presidential staffs. Hartmann, whose official title was "counselor to the president," was an absolute Ford loyalist who saw Rumsfeld and Cheney as Nixon men who had, either by luck or by cunning, survived the collapse of the previous presidency. Hartmann referred to Rumsfeld and Cheney as "the Praetorian guard" or "the little Praetorians," a reference to the palace guards whose determination to perpetuate their own power undermined the later Caesars of the Roman Empire.

Ford liked and trusted Hartmann, and he enjoyed tossing around ideas with his well-informed and well-balanced aide. So the president and his counselor took advantage of a physical quirk of the White House. There was a room to the side of the Oval Office, and Hartmann moved into it. That made him the only Ford aide who, without having to go through secretaries and schedulers, had instant and constant access to the president. This was inconvenient for Rumsfeld and Cheney, as their schemes were often thwarted when Hartmann got to Ford before they did. What to do? Cheney took charge of the most minute details of White House planning, even sending memos, which can be found in the file boxes at the Gerald Ford Library, about "the drainage problem in the sink in the first floor bathroom." This was typical of Cheney, who made it his business to show up early, stay late, and insinuate himself into every decision, no matter how seemingly inconsequential. Mastering the details of White House housekeeping proved to be a brilliant strategic move, as it enabled Cheney and Rumsfeld to move Hartmann out of the way, literally and politically. As James Mann notes, "Rumsfeld dealt with Hartmann through a housekeeping maneuver: He argued successfully that Hartmann's office should be turned into a private presidential study. Hartmann moved out, lost his proximity to Ford and was gradually marginalized."

With Hartmann disposed of, Rumsfeld and Cheney then went after a far more prominent player in the Ford White House, Henry Kissinger. Kissinger, who had come out of the Nixon administration with an undeserved Nobel Peace Prize and a somewhat more undeserved reputation as a master of statecraft, was at the peak of his power during the last years of the Nixon presidency, and he was able to maintain that power into the first year or so of the Ford presidency. Playing on Ford's awareness that he (Ford) knew a lot more about what was going on in Grand Rapids than in Moscow or Beijing, Kissinger convinced the new president to effectively cede charge of foreign policy to him as Ford's secretary of state and national security adviser. Writing about the Ford White House in 1975, novelist John Hersey recalled, "This president, who had a minimum exposure to foreign affairs before he came to office, hears, I am told, only one voice, and a mercurial voice it is, Henry Kissinger." Rumsfeld and Cheney, who despite their lack of significant foreign affairs experience had begun to fancy themselves as players on the world stage, did not enjoy surrendering authority for such a substantial sector of the presidential brief to anyone. And they were especially displeased about ceding that authority to Kissinger, whom Cheney in particular had come to see as too soft in the face of what he perceived as a still significant Soviet threat.

Though Cheney sought to keep the low profile that earned him his Secret Service code name of the mid 1970s, "Backseat," it was becoming increasingly clear that he was a right-winger, especially when it came to the cold war. "Whenever his private ideology was exposed, he appeared somewhat to the right of Ford, Rumsfeld, or, for that matter, Genghis Khan," observed Robert Hartmann. And right-wingers did not approve of Kissinger's efforts to ease tensions between the United States and the Soviet Union and China. When Kissinger and Nixon began to preach the doctrine of détente in the early 1970s, they faced a minor revolt among conservative Republicans. In 1972, Congressman John Ashbrook of Ohio, an unreconstructed cold warrior, challenged Nixon in the Republican primaries, winning little attention and few votes. But years later, as a cabinet secretary and vice president of the United States, Cheney would go out of his way to attend events honoring Ashbrook. During the Ford presidency, Cheney honored Ashbrook in another way: by attacking Kissinger and détente at every turn. In what former White House press secretary Ron Nessen described as "a behind the scenes struggle to curb the power of Kissinger," Cheney became a point man for his own ideology and Rumsfeld's ambition. He sent around a memo grumbling about how the failure of Ford to meet with Soviet writer Aleksandr Solzhenitsyn in 1975 fed "the illusion that all of a sudden we're bosom buddies with the Russians." He helped Rumsfeld inflate incidents that might embarrass Kissinger—minor or major—into crises. He joined the chief of staff in suggesting that Kissinger was mishandling the withdrawal from Vietnam and in arguing that with the 1976 presidential election approaching, Ford needed to foster the impression that he, not Kissinger, was in charge of the country's foreign policy. The constant carping worked. For Ford, as John Newhouse explained in his book *War and Peace in the Nuclear Age,* "policy and presidential politics had converged." Prodded by warnings from Rumsfeld and Cheney that a Republican primary challenge from former California governor Ronald Reagan would batter the administration for choosing détente over security, Ford began to see Kissinger as a liability. Early in November 1975, just weeks before Reagan's formal announcement of candidacy, Ford asked Kissinger to give up his responsibilities as national security adviser and simply serve as secretary of state. That meant Kissinger would no longer be calling the shots on both security and foreign intelligence matters. As part of the shuffle, Ford also obtained the resignation of hawkish secretary of defense James Schlesinger. To replace Schlesinger, Ford selected Rumsfeld, who had been angling for a cabinet appointment since 1968. Though the prospect of controlling the Pentagon appealed to Rumsfeld—according to the *New Republic's* John Osborne, Rumsfeld "wanted an assignment with a political future and White House staff jobs, however exalted, seldom offered that"—the chief of staff worried about leaving the West Wing at the point when he had finally beaten Kissinger and slowed the pace of détente.

Rumsfeld quickly calculated that he could enjoy the best of both worlds by convincing Ford to select Cheney, who was then just thirty-four, as the youngest White House chief of staff in history. So when talk turned to who would replace him as chief of staff, Rumsfeld asked, "What about Dick?" Some Ford aides joked that the media would inquire, "Who the hell is Dick Cheney?" But Cheney, finally beginning to move out from under Rumsfeld's shadow, delighted in his new power and prestige. When Ford traveled to China, both Kissinger and Cheney went along. Years later in a historical discussion involving former chiefs of staff, Cheney gleefully recalled, "The advance team, who worked for me, had given me a bigger bedroom, a bigger suite, than Henry had gotten. It was closer to the president. Henry didn't like that."

Cheney's poking at Kissinger as well as the secretary of state's highest-ranking ally in the administration, Vice President Nelson Rockefeller, inspired fears that the essentially untested chief of staff was not exactly the most seasoned political player. The fears were well-placed. As James Mann observed in *Rise of the Vulcans,* "Cheney's ascent in the Ford White House served as an illustration of how an individual can rise to the top by virtue of his willingness to take care of the mundane chores that persons with larger egos avoid, thereby establishing reliability and learning all the inner workings of an organization. Cheney was akin to the clerk who becomes chief executive, the copy editor who rises to become editor in chief, the accountant who takes over the film studio." Like any clerk who had chanced his way into the corner office, Cheney quickly mastered the surface-level Machiavellianism of rewarding friends and punishing enemies. He coordinated internal discussions about whether to use the threat of criminal indictments to scare the *New York Times* off stories about intelligence failures at a time when the Central Intelligence Agency and the shadowy networks of cold warriors that were associated with it had come under increased scrutiny. He plotted with a young consultant Rumsfeld had brought in, economist Arthur Laffer, to sell the president on supply-side economics—only to be blocked by Ford's chief economic adviser, the inevitable Alan Greenspan, who remained enamored of balanced budgets. Above all, Cheney continued the ceaseless chipping away at détente; when Robert Hartmann drafted a 1976 State of the Union address that echoed the official Ford administration line of support for efforts to improve relations with the Soviet Union, Cheney shoved it back at Hartmann with a note reading, "Bob—the foreign policy section is too tough on the Congress and not tough enough on the Russians." Securing superior suites than those given to the secretary of state, scheming to punish the press, getting jobs for political pals, and advancing kooky economic and diplomatic schemes: Cheney was in heaven.

Unfortunately, he was failing miserably at the only task that really mattered.

The prime responsibility, some would say "the sole responsibility," of a White House chief of staff in the run-up to a presidential election is to see that his boss remains in the White House. Unfortunately, it was a task for which Cheney, who had never run for public office himself and whose campaign experience did not extend much beyond holding the "button bag" for Warren Knowles on those trips around Wisconsin, was uniquely ill suited. Worse yet, Cheney was charged with managing the campaign of a president who, having inherited the office after his appointment as vice president, had never run for anything more than a safe Republican seat in the House of Representatives. It proved to be a politically deadly combination.

Scandalia

In 2004, when U.S. Supreme Court justice Antonin Scalia was urged to remove himself from a case involving Vice President Dick Cheney's energy task force, Scalia announced, "Since I do not believe my impartiality can reasonably be questioned, I do not think it would be proper for me to recuse."

The controversy started January 5, 2004, when Cheney gave Scalia a seat on the vice presidential plane, Air Force Two, and flew the conservative justice to Louisiana for a duck-hunting trip hosted by oil industry mogul Wallace Carline.

"The vice president and I were never in the same blind and never discussed the case," Scalia wrote in a twenty-one-page, "thou dost protest too much" defense of his decision to remain on the case. "Nor was I alone with him at any time during the trip, except perhaps for instances so brief and unintentional that I would not recall them—walking to or from a boat, perhaps, or going to or from dinner. Of course, we said not a word about the current case."

What Scalia didn't say was that some things can remain unsaid between two friends who have known each other for decades. In his extended apologia, Scalia acknowledged that in addition to being "an enthusiastic duck hunter," Cheney was a friend "with whom I am well acquainted." How well? Like many of the most powerful players in contemporary American public life—including

Secretary of Defense Donald Rumsfeld and Assistant Secretary of State Paul Wolfowitz—Scalia has known Cheney ever since their days working together in the administration of President Gerald Ford. As an assistant attorney general for the Office of Legal Counsel at the Ford Justice Department, Scalia was assigned to determine the legal ownership of tapes recorded during the presidency of Richard Nixon. In that role, Scalia was in frequent contact with Cheney, Ford's deputy chief of staff and then chief of staff.

The Sierra Club, which was suing for the release of Cheney's records of secret meetings with energy industry insiders such as Enron's Ken Lay, objected. "Justice Scalia misses the point. There's a problem when a justice and a litigant meet secretly at a private hunting retreat—regardless of what happens behind closed doors," explained club spokesman David Willett.

In fact, Willett was being rather too precise in his criticism. The federal law on recusal of jurists is much broader in scope and intent. It requires that "any jurist, judge or magistrate of the United States shall disqualify himself in any proceeding in which his impartiality might reasonably be questioned" (28 USC 455).

When the *New York Times* and other major daily newspapers argued in editorials that Scalia should step aside from the Cheney case—and when it seemed that every editorial cartoonist worth his pen-and-ink set was making light of the jurist's duck-blind defense—it was obvious that the "might reasonably be questioned" standard had been met. Yet Scalia, who manages the right-wing faction that dominates the High Court, did not choose to sanction himself.

This was not, of course, the first time Scalia had chosen not to remove himself from a case that was of pressing interest to Dick Cheney. In December 2000, when two of his sons were working for law firms that were doing legal work for the Bush-Cheney campaign, Scalia led the court majority that decided to shut down the recount of ballots cast in Florida's closely contested presidential voting. That 5–4 decision locked in a dubious 537-vote "lead" for Bush and Cheney, securing the vice presidency for Scalia's friend of a quarter century. Shortly thereafter, one of Scalia's sons was appointed to a top position in the Bush-Cheney administration's Department of Labor.

Was Scalia influenced by the prospect that a Bush-Cheney victory would benefit one of his children and one of his oldest friends? Of course not, he said. So it came as no surprise that he rejected the notion that a duck hunting trip with that friend should be viewed with concern. "If it is reasonable to think that a Supreme Court justice can be bought so cheap, the nation is in deeper trouble than I had imagined," Scalia argued in defending his decision to take the trip with Cheney.

The trouble with that statement is that no one seriously thought Scalia would exchange his vote for a duck-hunting trip. Rather, the concern involved the most basic of ethical questions: whether a jurist can impartially decide the case of a long-standing friend and ideological comrade. A responsible reading of the ethics code would seem to make it clear that Scalia ought not be deciding cases involving his admitted friend of three decades, Dick Cheney. After all, in the case of *Liteky v. United States,* 510 U.S. 540, 548 (1998), the High Court ruled that recusal was required where "impartiality might reasonably be questioned." The Court set a high standard, holding that what matters "is not the reality of bias or prejudice, but its appearance." The author of that decision? Justice Antonin Scalia.

Electorally unsophisticated and ideologically immature, Cheney made the mistake of trusting his instincts. The trouble was that they were consistently wrong. The long memos Ford's young chief of staff wrote on primary strategies, managing the Republican National Convention, and running against Democrat Jimmy Carter document Cheney's agonizing attempts to guide the campaign by stating the obvious while, consistently, missing the necessary nuances of the politically volatile post-Watergate moment. For instance, Cheney actually believed that downsizing Kissinger's role in the White House would placate conservatives who despised the secretary of state in particular and détente in general. Cheney did not understand until it was too late that Kissinger, with his flare for self-promotion, still seemed to be in charge. According to Howard "Bo" Callaway, the failed Georgia gubernatorial candidate who was the initial chair of the Ford campaign, Republican activists mistook the Cabinet-level shifts implemented by Ford at the behest of Rumsfeld and

Cheney as a defeat for conservatives. After all, Kissinger was still running the State Department, and James Schlesinger, a cold warrior popular with the GOP cadres, had been forced out of the Defense Department. "How can we defend a candidate who fired Dr. Schlesinger and said he will retain Dr. Kissinger if he is elected president?" asked Ronald Reagan. Instead of heading off a challenge from Reagan in the Republican primaries, the cabinet reshuffle had emboldened the Right.

As the campaign heated up in the late winter and spring of 1976, Reagan openly peddled the fantasy that Ford and Kissinger had allowed the Soviets to achieve military superiority. "Mr. Ford and Mr. Kissinger ask us to trust their leadership. Well, I find that more and more difficult to do. Henry Kissinger's recent stewardship of U.S. foreign policy has coincided precisely with the loss of U.S. military supremacy." Instead of countering Reagan's absurd claims, Cheney and other aides counseled Ford to avoid a fight over the issue. At precisely the point when Ford needed to flex whatever foreign policy muscles he had, the president was sent out to deliver the vapid feel-good speeches of a presumed front-runner. Thus, while Reagan stormed across the South decrying Ford and Kissinger for preparing to "give away" the Panama Canal, Ford appeared in Charlotte to declare: "I regret that some people in this country have disparaged and demeaned the role of the homemaker. I say—and I say with emphasis and conviction—that homemaking is good for America." Reagan's challenge, which should have been easily dispatched, was picking up steam. Faced with the prospect that he was managing the president to defeat—the influential conservative columnists Robert Novak and Rowland Evans observed, "White House Chief of Staff Richard Cheney . . . is blamed by Ford insiders for a succession of campaign blunders"—Cheney embarked on a course of action that he frequently would employ in the future: he pointed the finger of blame at others. The hapless Bo Callaway, who should have been removed from the campaign chairmanship months before, was finally fired by Cheney. But the chief of staff botched the transition, offering the job to Stuart Spencer, a strategist who turned it down, and creating what Reagan biographer Lou Cannon referred to as "a distraction that put the White House rather than the Reagan campaign on the defensive." Reagan started winning key primaries, beginning a remarkable surge that carried him all the way to the Republican National Convention in Kansas City, where Ford prevailed only barely, by a delegate vote of 1,187–1,070. As the convention approached, Cheney sought to calm the uprising on the right by bartering away Ford's foreign policies in a fruitless attempt to appeal to conservative southerners. When North Carolina senator Jesse Helms demanded a platform plank that denounced the 1975 Helsinki Agreement, which Ford had signed, the president complained that the move "added up to nothing less than a slick denunciation of administration foreign policy." But Cheney convinced him to accept the plank. Indeed, Cannon noted, "on every issue that the press might have interpreted as a conservative victory, Ford's people simply capitulated." Thus, while Ford was nominated, the convention ended in what was broadly seen as a symbolic win for Reagan and the Right—and, though this was little noted at the time, for Cheney's view that the genuinely moderate Ford could win only as a conservative. In what Robert Hartmann referred to as "the bedrock disagreement between the Praetorians and the handful of us who stubbornly resisted them," Cheney had prevailed. Ford, the old football star, would run right, not up the middle.

There are those who, knowing Cheney's Genghis Khan ideology, still suspect that he secretly schemed to move Ford and the Republican Party to the right. But that's a misread of how Cheney saw himself in 1976 and, at least to some extent, how he still sees himself today. He is a militant ideologue. But above all, Dick Cheney is a pursuer of power. There is no record of him ever putting principle ahead of loyalty to his own political advancement. That's why Cheney did not jump with other conservatives onto the Reagan bandwagon in 1976 or, for that matter, in 1980. He was already on the inside, and he wanted to stay there. This does not mean, however, that Cheney's extreme views did not play a significant role in Ford's loss to Democrat Jimmy Carter in the fall. As it happens, Cheney's conservativism doomed Ford.

Rumsfeld and Cheney believed, wrongly, that Vice President Rockefeller was a political liability. The nation's most prominent liberal Republican, Rockefeller had won the governorship of New York State four times, beating Averell Harriman, Franklin Roosevelt Jr., and former U.S. Supreme Court justice Arthur Goldberg, among others. He had mounted serious campaigns for the Republican nomination for the presidency in 1964 and 1968 and could point to a national base of support that extended far beyond New York and, as his track record of winning Democratic and independent votes indicated, beyond the boundaries of the Republican Party. When Ford assumed the presidency, his selection of Rockefeller to serve as his vice president was hailed as "a masterly political act" by the *New York Times*. And so it was. Unfortunately, Rumsfeld and Cheney saw Rockefeller as a rival within the Ford White House. Just as they fretted over Kissinger's dominance of foreign policy debates, so they feared Rockefeller would steer the administration's domestic agenda. Cheney was obsessed with undermining Rockefeller. Years later, Cheney griped, "In the Ford administration, we had major problems in managing the vice presidential relationship. . . . President Ford put the vice president in charge of all domestic policy making, put him in charge of the Domestic Council, gave him the assignment of creating policy, and let him staff the operation out." Each time Rockefeller came forward with a plan to address health care, education, or economic issues, Cheney said he saw it as his responsibility to be "the sand in the gears," making sure that the vice president's proposals were "shot down." "I was the SOB, and on a number of occasions, got involved in shouting matches with the vice president," Cheney told a forum organized by *Washington Monthly*. "[Rockefeller] finally told Ford at one point that the only way he would serve in a second Ford administration as vice president was if he could also be chief of staff." But Rumsfeld and Cheney had already decided that there would be no place for Rockefeller in a second Ford administration.

"The little Praetorians" were determined to get Rockefeller off the 1976 ticket. They constantly fed Ford reports suggesting that Rockefeller would drive Republican conservatives into the Reagan camp and, ultimately, weaken the ticket in the South come November. In fact, the conservatives were already going with Reagan, and Rockefeller would have benefited the ticket in November. But in what he would later describe as "one of the few cowardly things I did in my life," a reluctant Ford agreed in the fall of 1975 to demand that Rockefeller withdraw his name from consideration for the Republican vice presidential nomination. ("I didn't take myself off the ticket, you know—he asked me to do it," Rockefeller explained.) Instead of strengthening Ford's position, the president's poll numbers plummeted.

According to John Osborne, the White House watcher for

the *New Republic* during the Ford years, Rockefeller would always blame Cheney and Rumsfeld, not merely for forcing him
off the ticket, but for assuring Ford's defeat. The hatred was mu-
tual. Cheney arranged to have the amplifier systems turned down
when the vice president addressed Republican events. At the
Republican National Convention, where northeastern delegates
rounded up by Rockefeller finally secured the nomination for
Ford, Cheney tried to deny the vice president a place on the
podium with Ford. Rockefeller was so furious with Cheney that
he declared, "I am not going to have anything further to do with
[Ford's] campaign. . . . I am finished!" As it turned out, it was the
ticket made up of Ford and a suitably conservative running mate,
Kansan Bob Dole, that was finished. Cheney's strategy of moving
the party to the right in order to secure the South was a complete
failure. Democrat Jimmy Carter, the former Georgia governor,
won every state of the old Confederacy except Virginia. Yet the
election was still one of the closest in American history. Despite a
fall campaign characterized by frequent and embarrassing missteps, Ford had swept the West and held his own in New England
and the Great Lakes states. In the electoral college, he trailed
Carter 297–240. Ford would have won if he could have reversed
his narrow loss in a single state with forty-one electoral votes:
Nelson Rockefeller's New York. Cheney had blown it, managing
Ford to a defeat that could have been avoided. "It was the biggest
political mistake of my life," Ford would say of the decision to jet-
tison Rockefeller.

Actually, it was the second biggest mistake of his political life.
The first was to trust Dick Cheney and the lesser Praetorians to
steer his 1976 campaign.

Mr. No: As a member of Congress during the Reagan era, Cheney established a voting record that put him to the right of Reagan and Newt Gingrich. Cheney voted against the Endangered Species Act, the Clean Water Act, and the Clean Air Act; against funding nutrition programs for children; against the Federal Immunization Program; against a ban on armor-piercing bullets; against Head Start; against the Equal Rights Amendment; and against a call for Nelson Mandela's release from prison. (1982: with Reagan and Senator Malcolm Wallop)

CHAPTER 4

APARTHEID'S CONGRESSMAN

In Congress, for example, nobody's responsible for what Congress does or doesn't do. They're just responsible for their individual votes.

—Dick Cheney, 2000

Cheney's voting record was slightly more conservative than mine.

—Former House Speaker Newt Gingrich, 2000, referring to Dick Cheney's congressional service

[Cheney's] been against the Equal Rights Amendment and for apartheid in South Africa. . . .

—Former U.S. representative Patricia Schroeder, 2000

Trivia.

—Dick Cheney, 2000, describing questions about his votes against measures opposing apartheid

It is not the practice of Nelson Mandela to speak ill of other prominent players on the world stage, but he will make an exception for Dick Cheney.

Mandela is a courtly and gracious man who, even in the most challenging of circumstances, recognizes that as a Nobel Peace

Prize winner and former president of South Africa, he must be measured in his pronouncements regarding the men and women who govern the great nations of the world. But it is more than that. Mandela has always been nuanced in his observations of presidents and prime ministers, recognizing that even when someone does not appear to be an overt ally, he may yet be a covert comrade. The first time I interviewed Mandela, in the early 1990s, I was struck by the fact that he rarely missed an opportunity to praise President George Herbert Walker Bush. Mandela recognized that while the senior Bush was never an antiapartheid campaigner, he had not been, like former U.S. president Ronald Reagan or former British prime minister Margaret Thatcher, an aggressive apologist for the racist regimes that killed, maimed, and imprisoned members of the African National Congress (ANC). Mandela believed that when Bush replaced Reagan as president in 1989, the United States began sending different signals to the South African government, which early in Bush's term released Mandela and other jailed ANC leaders. The elder Bush had, in fact, been the first world leader to speak with Mandela upon the ANC leader's release. So the South African leader always had a kind word for Bush. But that did not mean he was enthusiastic about the people who surrounded the American president. When I mentioned to him that many Americans might be surprised to learn that he had warm feelings for a Republican president, he smiled and then noted that he was far less enthusiastic about Bush's secretary of defense. "I not so happy with Mr. Cheney," said Mandela.

Indeed, few figures get so great a rise out of Mandela as the man who is now the vice president of the United States.

Mandela refers to Cheney as "a dinosaur" and "an arch-conservative." Even as he criticized George W. Bush's rush to war in Iraq in 2003, Mandela suggested that the younger Bush was misguided. And the person misguiding him, Mandela suggested, was Cheney. The vice president, argued Mandela, did not want Bush "to belong to the modern age."

What is it that causes Mandela, who has befriended his jailers, forgiven his foes, and shared a Nobel Prize with the leader of the last apartheid government, to express antipathy toward Cheney? Is he simply a good judge of human nature? Perhaps. But the former South African president is, as well, an able analyst of the actions of public men. And he well recalls that when the notoriously secretive and closeted Dick Cheney was forced to record his true sentiments, he stood consistently on the side of the most reactionary, racist, and repulsive forces on the planet. Does Nelson Mandela worry about Dick Cheney being one heartbeat away from the presidency? "Well, there is no doubt," says the South African. "He opposed the decision to release me from prison."

Mandela is not exaggerating. He is reading the record from the one time Cheney was regularly pinned down on questions of race, class, war and peace, and, to borrow a phrase from George W. Bush, "good and evil." It is fair to say that among the many evil votes Cheney cast in Congress, the ten—count them, ten—separate votes he cast against moves to pressure South Africa to end apartheid were the worst. And the worst of those may well have been his 1986 vote against a resolution expressing the sense of the House that then president Ronald Reagan should demand that South Africa grant the immediate and unconditional release of Mandela and other political prisoners.

Yet aside from a brief flurry of attention immediately following his selection of himself as the Republican candidate for vice
president in 2000, Cheney has never been called to account for
his voting record in the House. Had he been, he would never
have been considered a viable contender for national office or a
serious player on the international stage. Indeed, it can fairly be
said that Cheney's voting record on foreign policy matters is
more frequently discussed in the media of Africa than that of the
United States.

That many Americans remain unaware of Cheney's ideological extremism provides ample evidence of the collapse of serious
political journalism in the United States. Cheney frequently
complains about the media, but when it comes to his darkest
choices, he has gotten a virtual free ride from the chattering
classes that parse politics in the United States. Cheney's record as
a member of the House of Representatives during a ten-year period from 1979 to 1989 is often analyzed by American observers
on the basis of his cordial relations with fellow members of Congress. News reports in the days following Cheney's selection of
himself to join Bush on the 2000 Republican ticket reflected
back on Cheney's decade in the House and described him as "an
insightful, thoughtful, straightforward, unflappable legislator"
who "has the temperament to be president." One article in a
Philadelphia newspaper portrayed him as "a friendly, gentlemanly candidate who is not an ideologue." Reading his press
clippings, you'd think Cheney was a regular Mr. Congeniality.
But Cheney was never the moderate "nice guy" that the spin
machine made him out to be. "He's able to appear so cool and ra-
tional, but there's this other side," a congressional aide who dealt
with Cheney during the fights over funding of the contra forces
that sought to overthrow the government of Nicaragua, ex-

plained to Phil McCombs, the *Washington Post* staff writer who was one of the few journalists ever to write seriously about Cheney. "There was a harshness, that sneer he'd get, sort of attributing bad motives to his opponents, that you were suspect, that you were pro-Communist. There was venom—he made some very vicious remarks. He scares me." For all the attempts to portray him as an affable legislator with an eye toward compromise, the truth is that Cheney had little respect for the Congress or its members; even when he served in the House, he fought to undermine the ability of the legislative branch to hold the executive accountable. Almost as soon as he left the chamber to become secretary of defense, a friend of Cheney's told *The New Yorker,* he began to refer to his former colleagues as "a bunch of annoying gnats." Above all, Cheney was an ideologue. Several years into his House tenure, the *Washington Post* referred to him as a "moderate." Instead of celebrating his luck at having kept his extreme views under the radar of the national press, Cheney ordered an aide to contact the *Post* and demand a correction. The aide, Dave Gribben, recalled that Cheney said, "Will you please call the *Post* and tell them I'm a conservative? Don't they check my voting record? I've got a voting record and they ought to look at it."

Okay, let's look at the record. Out of 435 members of the House, Dick Cheney was:

- one of four who voted against the Undetectable Firearms Act of 1988, a measure written to prohibit the production and importation of plastic guns and other weapons containing so little metal that they would not set off metal detectors. Concerns about the prospect that terrorists could sneak firearms onto airplaces and into public buildings led even the most avid supporters of the National Rifle Association agenda to vote for the legislation, but not Cheney.

- one of eight who, in 1987, opposed renewing the Older Americans Act providing nutrition and support services for the elderly. Had Cheney's extreme position prevailed, the $1.6 billion program, one of the primary programs to assure that older Americans do not go hungry, would have been effectively shut down.

- one of eight who, in 1987, opposed reauthorization of the Federal Immunization Program, which reimbursed states for the cost of providing vaccinations to children.

- one of eight who, in 1987, opposed reauthorization of the Clean Air Act.

- one of nine who opposed the Environmental Research, Development, and Demonstration Act of 1984, which allocated close to $300 million annually for Environmental Protection Agency studies on environmental risks to public health and safety.

- one of nine who, in 1987, opposed reauthorizing the Health Service Corps, the program that paid the educational costs of doctors who agreed to serve in medically underserved inner cities and rural areas and on Indian reservations.

- one of nine who, in 1988, opposed allowing federal employees to take time off to care for sick family members.

To get isolated so frequently, and on such major issues, in the Less Than Ten Club in so large and ideologically diverse a legislative chamber as the 435-member U.S. House of Representatives was no easy task, especially for a former White House chief of staff who was, by virtue of his résumé, a high-profile member. Cheney's well-developed instinct for political preservation—which has always proven more powerful than his ideological impulses—might have been expected to move him to the left in any other political context. But Dick Cheney was voting with a purpose. His House votes were cast with an eye to increasing his credibility with the party's rising conservative bloc and, in so doing, to position himself to become the leader of the Republican caucus and, as quickly as possible, Speaker of the House. Though Cheney was comfortable with the ideology behind them, none of his House votes were crimes of political passion. Rather, they were coolly calculated "risks" taken in order to renew his political prospects—and the grasp on power that had been broken when he was forced to relinquish the chief of staff job. After he managed Ford to defeat in 1976, Cheney was damaged goods politically. He left the White House when Ford did and ended up back at Bradley, Woods & Company, the Washington investment advice firm to which he was exiled from the Nixon administration.

Cheney was desperate to get back into the political arena, but Jimmy Carter's Democrats controlled the White House, and there were few high-level positions for washed-up Ford advisers on Capitol Hill, where the Democratic "Watergate babies" were moving the House and Senate to the left. Even within the Republican Party, where Ronald Reagan was on the rise, Cheney's association with the more moderate Ford wing of the party was a liability. There was no easy road up.

Luckily for Cheney, Teno Roncalio was homesick.

The son of Italian immigrants whose father came to work the mines of Rock Springs—the Wyoming town where Cheney did his heavy drinking after washing out of Yale—Roncalio was a former aide to Wyoming Democratic senator Joseph C. O'Mahoney, an old-school western populist who defended the Constitution and doubted the wisdom of U.S. military adventures and entanglements abroad. Roncalio stood as the Democratic candidate for Wyoming's single U.S. House seat in 1964, the year Lyndon Johnson became the last Democratic presidential candidate to carry Wyoming. The Johnson landslide swept Roncalio into the House of Representatives, where he served as Wyoming's sole representative on and off until 1978. Roncalio was sometimes referred to as "Wyoming's last Democrat," and it is true that no Democrat has won a federal election in that state since he left office. But he was more popular than his party and might well have won another term in 1978. Certainly, no Washington insider like Dick Cheney, whose stiffness on the campaign trail is legendary, would have posed a serious threat to the personable and politically savvy Roncalio. But Teno, who was in his sixties, was tired of Congress. So he announced in 1977 that he was not going to seek another term.

Suddenly, Dick Cheney remembered how very much he had always wanted to represent Wyoming in the U.S. House of Representatives.

The Cheneys hightailed it out of Washington and set up housekeeping in Casper, the city they had abandoned a decade earlier. If Dick could get himself elected to Congress, he would be back in the game. Indeed, the man who with his wife would write a forgettable text on Speakers of the House, *Kings of the Hill,* had determined that he could, and would, become the most powerful Republican on Capitol Hill. It was an audacious goal for a failed campaign manager who had never run for public office. But Cheney, whose one major project as a graduate student at the University of Wisconsin was a study of how House voting patterns were influenced by partisan pressures, believed that by making himself indispensable to party leaders and by positioning himself in the right place ideologically, he could achieve it. And he very nearly did, thanks in no small measure to all those radically right-wing votes. Chastened by the challenge of the Reaganites in 1976, Cheney had come to understand that the Republican Party was beginning a long march to the right. It was clear that conservatives would soon be calling the shots in the Grand Old Party, so the chief of staff of the country's last genuinely moderate Republican president set out to remake himself as the meanest conservative of them all. It would take some work for Cheney to convince conservatives that he was one of them— although savvy observers, such as Ford aide Robert Hartmann, had recognized years earlier that Cheney genuinely was of the tribe—but first he would have to convince the people of Wyoming that he was one of them.

While Wyoming voters had read Dick Cheney's name in the papers, they did not know him well. The slick campaign brochures distributed by his unusually well-financed 1978 campaign featured the headline WHO IS DICK CHENEY AND WHY IS HE RUNNING FOR CONGRESS? What little folks in Wyoming did know of Cheney, they did not particularly like. The state's Republicans had bristled in 1976, for instance, when he had pressured them to back Ford, the Washington insider from east of the Mississippi, over Reagan, the westerner, for the party's presidential nomination. Cheney's first challenge in 1978 was to win the Republican nomination against two "local" candidates who referred to him as a carpetbagger. State Treasurer Ed Witzenburger and Jack Gage, the son of a prominent Wyoming politico, asked one logical question: Wasn't Dick Cheney just using Wyoming to get a new job in Washington? Cheney countered the question by explaining that he was a VIR (very important Republican) with national connections that would allow him to do more for Wyoming in Washington. Campaign materials so inflated Cheney's record that journalist Lou Cannon noted while reporting on the campaign that it sounded as if "Gerald Ford had helped Cheney run the country." Cheney smiled and said, "That's a fair comment."

Cannon, one of Cheney's favorite journalists, interpreted the comment as an attempt at humor. But Cheney was running a very serious campaign. There was nothing fun or frivolous about the ambitious thirty-seven-year-old's plan to get his political career back on track. There was nothing populist about his program or his people-to-people skills. His campaign appearances were described as being "like seminars." And his poll numbers were not particularly good. According to Cannon, Cheney had "less name recognition than he would have liked," and Witzenburger, who had actually won a statewide race, was coming on strong.

Then, Cheney was blessed with his first heart attack. For most men, a heart attack at age thirty-seven would be a troubling development. But for someone with Dick Cheney's ambitions, his health problems became a perfect campaign prop. "The complete coverage of the heart attack and Cheney's recovery from it solved the [name recognition] problem," explained Cannon. Even before he was fully recovered from the minor attack, the candidate faked a mock campaign committee called Cardiacs for Cheney to exploit the sympathy vote. In a two-page letter, which he claimed was written from his sickbed, Cheney informed Republican voters that he was giving up his three-pack-a-day smoking habit and that he would carry on with the campaign because it had given him a "sense of purpose." The tactic worked. Cheney won the Republican primary easily and went on to face Democrat Bill Bagley, a fourth-generation Wyoming native and former Roncalio aide whose campaign manager pointed out, "Wyoming has always been Cheney's second choice. When he ran into difficulty in college, he came back to Wyoming. When he was out of work after Ford lost, he came to Wyoming." The criticism was on point, and in another year it might have resonated. But in 1978, with President Carter's approval rating falling to 25 percent in the state, where Democratic environmental and energy policies were portrayed as a "war on the West," a Republican surge carried Cheney to victory. Two years after Ford's defeat, the former White House chief of staff was headed back to Washington as a freshman congressman.

Cheney had lost ground to make up. So he moved fast, but this time he did so far more strategically than he had in the Nixon and Ford White Houses. No longer clinging to Donald Rumsfeld's coattails, Cheney was finally gaining the competence he had lacked as a young White House aide. He was, as well, developing real connections to the party's financial overseers—from a seat on the Interior Committee, which had authority over mining and drilling issues, he began collecting substantial campaign contributions from the oil and gas industries. Cheney's most valuable asset, however, was his road map for acquiring power in the House itself. In *Kings of the Hill,* the 1983 book he wrote with Lynne Cheney about Speakers of the House, Cheney detailed the courses that past Speakers had charted in pursuit of power. The constant he identified was a willingness to take on complicated tasks and unappealing responsibilities that were essential to the party. Cheney would do the same.

By the time he was in his second term, the forty-year-old congressman had assumed on the relatively thankless task of chairing the House Republican Policy Committee. This was the perfect job for someone who intended to rise as an inside-the-party man, and Cheney was remaking himself as the perfect right-wing Republican. As the new Reagan administration was breaking old patterns of bipartisanship in favor of a more ideological approach to governance, Cheney positioned himself as an essential point man for the White House and its conservative allies in Congress. "Whenever there was a closed-door meeting on Capitol Hill where congressional Republicans were working out their policies or strategy, Cheney was probably inside," notes journalist and historian James Mann.

Like his colleague and sometime competitor Newt Gingrich, Cheney correctly calculated that for Republicans to improve their position in the House, they would need to give the party the identity it had lacked during the 1970s. In its new guise, the GOP would become more rabidly conservative and radically cynical than ever before. The party of Abraham Lincoln and the abolitionists would embrace the remnants of the southern segregationist cause and the most intolerant theocrats; the party of Teddy Roosevelt and the trustbusters would become the political vehicle of the corporate consolidators and monopolists. And Dick Cheney would place himself where he liked best to be: be-

Lipstick Lynbian

Tired of politics? Let's open a romance novel. Mmmm, this looks like an interesting passage:

"Let us go away together, away from the anger and imperatives of men. There will be only the two of us and we shall linger through long afternoons of sweet retirement."

Flip the page. Here's one woman saying to another: "In the evenings I shall read to you while you work your cross-stitch in the firelight. And then we shall go to bed, our bed, my dearest girl."

And how about this scene, where our heroine notes, with no small measure of longing, "that the women in the cart had a passionate, loving intimacy forever closed to her. How strong it made them. What comfort it gave."

Goodness! Who is the author of this lesbian-friendly literature?

Why, it's the fabulous Mrs. Dick, Lynne Cheney. The former chairwoman of the National Endowment on the Humanities under Presidents Reagan and Bush, she was in the late 1980s a more prominent player in many Washington circles than her reserved husband. A better student (she actually finished a doctorate in English, which explored Kant's influence on the poetry of Matthew Arnold) and a better public speaker (no right-wing group ever complains when Dick's "better half" has to pinch-hit for him), Lynne Cheney is one of the country's most outspoken cultural conservatives.

Long before Dan Quayle discovered "Murphy Brown" was pregnant, Lynne Cheney was ranting about moral decay. Don't even get her started on the subject of racy movies or rap music. So what gives with the lesbian lit?

Lynne Cheney's not talking. Her White House biography makes no mention of *Sisters,* the book from which the preceding passages are borrowed. When a *New York Times* reporter asked America's Second Lady about *Sisters,* Cheney, who is also the author of a book titled *American Memory,* claimed she could not remember the plot. (Lynne's selective memory, a condition common among cultural conservatives caught out in the vast wasteland, is shared by her husband. Just ask him about all those weapons of mass destruction [WMDs] in Iraq.)

Lynne Cheney penned *Sisters,* a torrid tome that explores brothels, rape attempts, and lesbian love in the wild west, in 1981, when her husband was a second-term congressman. There was a demand then for sexy historical novels, and Lynne Cheney was going to fill it. What made *Sisters* different from the more typical tales of swashbuckling pirates and damsels in distress was its fascination with girl-girl action. The book cover promised to take readers into "a world where women were treated as decorative figurines or as abject sexual vassals . . . where wives were led to despise the marriage act and prostitutes pandered to husbands' hungers . . . where the relationship between women and men became a kind of guerilla warfare in which women were forced to band together for the strength they needed and at times for the love they wanted."

Talk-radio host Laura Flanders, the author of *Bush-women: Tale of a Cynical Species,* offers a more succinct blurb. *Sisters,* she says, is "a whole book where [Cheney] gloried in lesbian love affairs."

Flanders's review: "[*Sisters*] is a breathy, gothic romance, horribly written. It celebrates lesbian love and promotes the value of preventive devices, condoms, to women who want to remain free. It features a woman who has unmarried sex with the widow of her sister—all this by Lynne Cheney, the cultural warrior of the right."

Unfortunately for Mrs. Dick, the book wasn't a best seller—Lynne Cheney said in an interview some years ago that it sold about five hundred copies—proving that standards had not sunk quite as low as Cheney and other cultural conservatives feared. Undeterred, Cheney would take another shot at the fiction market with a novel titled *Executive Privilege,* in which a vice president suffers countless indignities. (Let's not even go there.)

Since her husband took over the government, however, Lynne Cheney's gone legit. She's written a best-selling book for kids, *America: A Patriotic Primer,* and she even sponsors a literary prize, the James Madison Book Award, to recognize the best history texts written for children. History's a big deal for Lynne Cheney. She's a crusader for improving American heritage curriculums. But when it comes to her own history, Lynne Cheney was forced to draw the line.

Early in 2004, after the New York Theatre Workshop satirized *Sisters* in performances that featured actors reading the racier passages, New American Library, an imprint of the Penguin Group, proposed to republish Cheney's out-of-print novel. The publisher was betting that there would be a good deal more interest in the book, considering both the heightened prominence of the Cheneys and the fact that their daughter Mary was one of the country's best-known lesbians.

The Cheneys were, by all accounts, cool with Mary's sexuality. Like many Washington Republicans, their social conservatism crusading was just an act for the Christian Coalition crowd. Mr. Dick even took a tolerant view of same-sex marriage proposals during his 2000 vice presidential debate with Joe Lieberman. "People should be free to enter into any kind of relationship they want to enter into," argued the Republican candidate, who added that the states—not the federal government—should decide whether to allow gay and lesbian couples to marry.

Unfortunately, as the 2004 election campaign heated up, the White House political team needed to pump up its poll numbers with religious right voters who saw same-sex unions as sinful. So George Bush came out for a constitutional amendment banning them. That put Dick Cheney in the position of having to choose between Bush and his daughter. It was no contest: Bush won. And with Dick falling on his sword, Lynne Cheney had to do the same.

The publisher got a call from Lynne's lawyer. *Sisters* is back in the closet.

hind the curtains, where the dirty work was done. As he moved up the hierarchy of the House Republican Caucus—where the directionless minority leader, Bob Michel, would soon come to refer to the Wyoming congressman as "my right arm"—Cheney became ever more central to the conservative enterprise. While he worked well with more moderate Republicans in the House—recognizing that as long as they were around, they would be casting votes in leadership races—he prodded right-wingers to run for open seats and backed them over more mainstream contenders; in 1986, for instance, he was the only prominent Republican in the country to endorse supply-side guru Arthur Laffer in a California U.S. Senate primary. Laffer lost, but many of the candidates Cheney encouraged won. And as the 1980s wore on, Cheney surfed the rising right-wing tide. In 1987, he was elected chair of the House Republican Conference. A year later, he was chosen as House Republican whip, making him the party's number two man in the chamber he had joined only a decade earlier. The myth makers who pen official biographies have written the story of Cheney's quick ascent within the House in a way that fosters the fantasy that he moved up solely because of superior skills. For reasons that should be obvious, they neglect the ideological component that was far more determinative. Cheney distinguished himself at a time when conservatives were coming on strong by establishing impeccable right-wing credentials.

In Ronald Reagan's Washington, the action was on the right, and so was Dick Cheney. Unfortunately, he ended up on the wrong side of a lot of history—and he left a permanent record.

Cheney's congressional votes—the true measure of his House

"service"—were indeed those of the dinosaur and arch-conservative that Nelson Mandela described. How right-wing was Congressman Dick Cheney? He actually found a space to the right of Ronald Reagan. According to *Congressional Quarterly,* Cheney echoed Reagan's stance only 79 percent of the time when the pair served together in Washington. But Cheney voted "conservative" 89 percent of the time. Translation: When Reagan veered to the left, Cheney remained on the right. Newt Gingrich, who was elected to the House with Cheney in 1978, said after they had both left the chamber: "Cheney's voting record was slightly more conservative than mine." So if Reagan and Gingrich were too liberal for Cheney, with whom did he make common cause? "In 10 years in the House," *Business Week* reported in a 1998 article, "[Cheney] chocked up a conservative voting record that rivaled Senator Jesse Helms." Helms, the North Carolina segregationist who went "respectable" with his election to the Senate in 1972, would never have been considered a credible candidate for president or vice president. Yet Dick Cheney cast the same votes and became vice president in name and president in reality.

When Bill Clinton got in trouble with an intern, his critics asked, "Where is the outrage?" Well, where was the outrage when Republicans nominated for the vice presidency a man, Cheney, who had:

- opposed reauthorization of the Endangered Species Act, the Clean Water Act, the Federal Water Pollution Act, and the Superfund to clean up hazardous waste sites; voted in 1986 against funding the Safe Drinking Water Act; voted in 1985 against requiring corporations to keep track of chemical emissions; voted in 1984 to eliminate the right of citizens to sue for enforcement of the Superfund law; and voted with just twenty-five other members in 1987 to uphold Reagan's veto of the Clean Water Act.

- voted against a ban on the manufacturing and importation of armor-piercing "cop killer" bullets; against limits on the interstate sale of shotguns and rifles; and against a seven-day waiting period for gun purchases.

- cast ten separate votes against funding nutrition programs for children, including one vote in 1983 (on which he was joined by just fifteen other House members) opposing a move to protect food programs for women and infants from budget cuts.

- voted against the 1984 Hunger Relief Act, which expanded eligibility for the federal food stamp program.

- voted in 1983 to raise the retirement age for Social Security recipients from sixty-five to sixty-seven, after declaring following the 1982 election that every Republican member of Congress was "committed to support Social Security to his dying breath."

- voted in 1983 to cap Social Security cost-of-living adjustments for retired Americans living on fixed incomes, but voted in 1988 against capping out-of-pocket expenses for Medicare recipients, establishing a record so bad that a Cox News Service headline once proclaimed SENIOR GROUPS CALL CHENEY'S VOTING RECORD A DISASTER.

- voted in 1982 against providing mortgage assistance for low-income home buyers.
- voted in 1988 to eliminate protections against housing discrimination for families with children.
- cast repeated votes against maintaining and funding Head Start programs.
- consistently opposed the creation of the Department of Education.
- voted in 1984 to cut off federal education assistance to public schools that prevented religious groups from using its facilities for prayer meetings.
- voted in 1985 to freeze funding for higher education programs.
- opposed reauthorization of college student aid programs contained in the Higher Education Act.
- voted repeatedly against programs to provide assistance to displaced workers.
- voted in 1985 against legislation requiring factory owners to notify employees before closing plants.
- voted in 1986 against "Buy American" legislation that would have required federal agencies to purchase goods and services from firms that employ U.S. workers.
- voted during the Reagan recession of the early 1980s to block extension of unemployment benefits and initiatives to provide health insurance for the unemployed and their families.
- voted in 1983 against the Equal Rights Amendment.
- voted to amend civil rights legislation to read "The term 'person' shall include unborn children from the

moment of conception" and earned a 100 percent antiabortion rating from the National Right to Life Committee.

- voted to support Reagan's veto of the Civil Rights Restoration Act of 1987.
- voted for a constitutional amendment to ban the use of busing to integrate public schools.
- voted in 1983 against authorizing a program designed to help local school districts offset the cost of desegregating public schools.
- voted in 1988 against Hate Crimes Data legislation that provided for the collection and publication of information regarding acts of violence that were linked to racial, religious, ethnic, or gender prejudices.
- voted in 1982 to fund a Reagan administration initiative to produce chemical weapons.
- voted consistently for legislation to fund the contra rebels seeking to overthrow the elected government of Nicaragua and against legislation to support peaceful efforts to end apartheid in South Africa.

Cheney's record caused a brief stir after he named himself as George W. Bush's running mate. But then the Republican spin machine started whirling. Gerald Ford and Bob Dole wrote a laudatory opinion piece in the *New York Times.* And television programs such as a July 26, 2000 editon of PBS's *NewsHour with Jim Lehrer* featured Cheney apologists like former congressman Vin Weber, a Minnesota Republican, who looked into the camera and said with a straight face: "Dick Cheney is one of the most respected political leaders in our country."

Referring to their time together in Congress, Weber said that Cheney was "the sort of person that everybody turned to for judgment, maturity, intellect, depth, and perspective on the issues." In reality, members of Congress had, on the most contentious issues of the 1980s, turned against Cheney, isolating him in the Less Than Ten Club. Yet, most of the media seemed to accept Cheney's dismissal of questions about his voting record as "trivia." The one issue that Weber and others could not seem to spin away was Cheney's stance regarding apartheid. When even President Bill Clinton expressed dismay about votes against legislation seeking the release of Mandela, Cheney decided that he had to address the issue.

There were no apologies. He did not, as writer Joe Conason suggested, "take responsibility for prolonging apartheid." Cheney defended his votes by saying, "The ANC was then viewed as a terrorist organization." Never mind that the United Nations, leaders of countries around the world, and the overwhelming majority of members of Congress had taken the side of the African National Congress at the time Cheney cast his votes against sanctioning South Africa's racist regime and seeking Mandela's release. The only olive branch Cheney offered critics of the aid and comfort he had given the apartheid rulers of segregated South Africa was to mumble that Mandela was "a great man." Cheney said he had grown more comfortable with Mandela because the ANC leader had "mellowed."

On that point, as on so many others, Cheney was wrong. Mandela had not mellowed on the subject of Cheney. Ask him about the vice president, and Mandela will state the truth: "The majority of the U.S. Congress was in favor of my release, and he opposed it." Even that, Mandela says, he might be able to forgive.

Contempt for Congress

Whenever Dick Cheney swears an oath to uphold the Constitution, it's a pretty safe bet that he's got his fingers crossed.

Cheney just can't abide by the separation of powers part. It gets in the way of presidents doing whatever they damn well please. And Cheney is a big damn well pleaser.

In 1990, before the first Gulf War, Cheney told then president George Herbert Walker Bush not to seek the approval of Congress for his plan to launch a war to remove Iraqi troops from Kuwait. The president chose not to take his secretary of defense's advice, and the House and Senate engaged in thoughtful and at times passionate debates a mere three days before the war was to begin. For the administration, the final votes were uncomfortably close, with the House giving its approval by a margin of 250–183 and the Senate doing so by just 52–47.

Cheney, who saw the last minute debates as a distraction from the serious work of going to war, vowed that when he ran the country things would operate differently.

In 2002, as the second Bush administration was planning for the second Gulf War, Cheney played it smoother. There would be no serious or sincere consultation of Congress. And there would be no eve-of-war debates this time.

In early September 2002, when White House aides

met to discuss the route to war, Cheney argued for having Congress vote sooner rather than later. He proposed squeezing Congress to vote in October 2002 on a resolution that was written to give the president a broad, ill-defined authorization to use force against Iraq. The idea was that with memories of the 9/11 terrorist attacks on the World Trade Center and the Pentagon still fresh in the minds of most Americans, and with midterm congressional elections approaching in November, Congress should be pressured to surrender its oversight responsibilities at an early stage in the discussion. Then the administration would not have to bother getting House and Senate approval for the actual war plan.

Wise members of Congress, like Vietnam-era veteran Jim McDermott, a Democrat from Washington State, recognized what Cheney and the other war planners were up to. "If we pass this resolution, we are setting precedents that we will regret: that America can start preemptive wars and that Congress can turn over authority to start a war to a president," he said. West Virginia senator Robert Byrd, the Constitution's most consistent defender in Congress, warned that "this resolution gives to the president—lock, stock, and barrel—the authority to use the military forces of this country however he will, whenever he will, and wherever he will, and for so long as he will."

But most members of Congress, Republicans and Democrats, noted the looming election date and voted to give the White House what it wanted.

The scheme worked, and as the war approached, Congress was effectively sidelined.

This was how Cheney liked it.

Even when he had served in Congress, Cheney championed the executive branch over the legislative branch. No one worked harder to weaken the authority of Congress to police the White House. As the ranking Republican member of the House Intelligence Committee in 1987, Cheney sought to defend the Reagan administration's dirty dealings in the Iran-contra affair. A passionate backer of the administration's schemes to "manage" Latin America with contras and coups, and a fierce foe of laws written by Congress to bar sales of weapons to rebel forces seeking to overthrow the government of Nicaragua, Cheney was required to justify the actions of Lieutenant Colonel Oliver North, Vice Admiral John Poindexter, and other Reagan administration aides who set up elaborate schemes to get money to the so-called contras. And he did his duty with gusto. Indeed, argues former White House counsel John Dean, "during the scandal, it should be recalled, Cheney became President Reagan's principal defender in Congress."

After it was revealed that members of Reagan's administration had peddled U.S. arms to Iran and then used the proceeds to fund the contras—in a scheme set up with the express purpose of circumventing congressional authority—House and Senate panels were initiated to investigate what was broadly viewed by Democrats and a number of Republicans as a constitutional crisis. Cheney, who served as vice chairman of the House Iran-Contra Committee, saw no crisis, however. While other members of the panels challenged North, Poindexter, and other accused conspirators to explain their actions, Cheney tossed them softballs.

During one hearing, Poindexter, who had served as Reagan's national security adviser, expressed skepticism that members of Congress could be trusted with information about covert actions. Cheney responded with the suggestion that "if the relationship is going to work long-term, there have to be a handful of members of Congress who have the knowledge about policy to do whatever needs to be done on the Hill to support and sustain the president's efforts downtown."

"I certainly agree with you, Mr. Cheney, that we need a better way," replied Poindexter, who added, "There needs to be greater acceptance of the fact that the president's power under the Constitution makes him the primary architect of foreign policy, and the American people have a chance every four years to confirm or deny that particular foreign policy." If Congress could accept that standard, Poindexter said, a few members could be brought into the loop, but "then other people in Congress ought to stay out of the issue."

Nodding, Cheney thanked the admiral for his presentation.

That exchange provided an indication of what was to come.

Most members of the House and Senate Iran-contra panels signed a majority report that found evidence of "secrecy, deception, and disdain for law" by the administration. But Cheney signed a minority report that dismissed the findings of the majority as "political guerrilla warfare." "The bottom line," claimed the minority report to which Cheney and seven other Republicans attached their names, "is that the mistakes of the Iran-Contra affair were just that—mistakes in judgment, and nothing more. There was no constitutional crisis, no systematic disrespect for 'the rule of law,' no grand conspiracy, and no Administration-wide dishonesty or coverup. In fact, the evidence will not support any of the more hysterical conclusions the committees' report tries to reach."

Even Republicans found the minority report embarrassing in its complete surrender to the administration. U.S. senator Warren Rudman, the New Hampshire Republican who served as vice chairman of the Senate Iran-contra panel, dismissed the minority report as "pathetic." Recalling a comment by former United Nations ambassador Adlai Stevenson about a similarly uninspired document, Rudman said, "This particular report is one in which the editors separated the wheat from the chaff and, unfortunately, it printed the chaff."

But Cheney, whom *Washington Post* columnist Mary McGrory described as "the intellectual leader of the know-nothings who gave us the minority report on the Iran-Contra scandal," wasn't giving up. He went on a crusade against proposals to renew separation-of-powers principles by strengthening congressional oversight of U.S. foreign policy. Foreshadowing the Bush-Cheney administration's penchant for dismissing legitimate criticism of its policies as partisan cheap shots, Cheney accused the Democrats of "overdramatizing [the Iran-contra scandal] for their own political purposes"—conveniently forgetting that some of the most prominent Republicans in the House and Senate had joined the Democrats in condemning the administration's assault on the Constitution. To Cheney's view, those who sought to give Congress a greater role in foreign policy were "prepared to undermine the presidency."

Early in 2003, as Cheney furthered his plan to marginalize Congress and launch a no-strings-attached preemptive war with Iraq, John Dean reflected back on the vice president's actions during the Iran-contra investigation and observed, "Clearly, Cheney wants greater powers for the presidency. . . .

"There is one problem, and it is spelled out in those sheets of parchment where the Framers laid out our system of government," explained Dean. "They rejected monarchy, even a temporary king or queen."

What he cannot forgive is the fact that Cheney has not changed. Mandela explains that he is concerned about Cheney not merely because of the American vice president's voting record in the 1980s, but because of his actions in the 2000s. "Quite clearly, we are dealing with an arch-conservative in Dick Cheney." And, Mandela says, what troubles him particularly is the prospect that it is not George W. Bush, but rather Dick Cheney, who is now "the real president of the United States of America."

Desk–chair warrior: As Secretary of Defense during the administration of George H.W. Bush, Cheney cashiered the possibility of a peace dividend coming from the fall of the Soviet Union. Then, working in secret, he generated a new defense plan that read like an imperialist manifesto, bluntly stating that "In the Middle East and Southwest Asia, our overall objective is to remain the predominant outside power in the region and preserve U.S. and western access to the region's oil." (1991)

CHAPTER 5

POCKETING THE PEACE DIVIDEND

We must hedge against the unexpected.
—Dick Cheney, 1993

Without a superpower enemy, the first hints of the openly—proudly—imperial role (the U.S.) would take on in the new century emerged, as the Pentagon, rather than declaring victory and demobilizing, began to test the waters in a variety of new capacities.
—Chalmers Johnson, 2004, describing Cheney's
focus as secretary of defense on maintaining
Cold War levels of military spending

As the last secretary of defense of the cold war era, Dick Cheney was handed a unique opportunity to guide not just the United States, but the world away from the brink of nuclear holocaust, away from the excessive military spending that was bankrupting superpowers and client states alike, and away from the fearmongering that had manipulated the peoples of the planet into seeing one another as threats rather than as neighbors. Cheney did not choose to exercise that option, however. Rather, the man who had worked so hard to undermine détente during the Ford administration determined that he would not allow a little development like the collapse of the Soviet Union to end the cold war.

Pragmatic as always, Cheney surveyed the state of the world in early 1989 and determined that there was no money to be made from peace, no political advantage to be gained from tranquillity, and no power to be accumulated in a post-superpower world.

While misguided historians suggest that Cheney's term as secretary of defense was a period of transition and transformation, it was, in fact, a time when the man at the top of the most powerful military-industrial complex in the history of the world struggled to maintain continuity. His success, achieved against all odds, would do more to define the future of the planet than all the best efforts of presidents, prime ministers, and successive secretaries-general of the United Nations. Against the looming threat of peace and prosperity, Dick Cheney assured that, in the words of Gore Vidal, the decades to come would be defined by "perpetual war." Cheney was as fervently anti-Communist as the next right-winger, but when Communist-led governments ceased to pose even the slightest challenge to the United States or its allies, the secretary of defense jettisoned the rationale for the cold war while maintaining the form and substance of the struggle. Did Cheney anticipate when he became secretary of defense that his tenure would yield such dramatic results? Of course not. As always, he was just hustling for power.

The collapse of Ronald Reagan's presidency into the embarrassment of the Iran-contra scandal and the uncertainty of the autumn 1987 stock market crash had made it clear that the promise of the Republican revolution that began with the Gipper's 1980 election as president had been thwarted. Republicans did maintain control of the White House in 1988, when George Herbert Walker Bush defeated the hapless Democratic candidacy of Michael Dukakis, but their control of the Senate had been lost in 1987, and their prospects for gaining a majority in the House seemed slimmer than ever in the days following the election of 1988. Convinced that the House Speakership for which he had spent a decade positioning himself would remain beyond his grasp for years to come, Cheney began to lose interest in Congress. This was actually his worst political miscalculation since he steered Gerald Ford toward the disastrous southern strategy of 1976; within just six years, the man to whom Cheney handed responsibility for forging a Republican renaissance in the House, a former college professor from Georgia named Newt Gingrich, would be Speaker. There are, of course, no guarantees that Cheney, who lacked Gingrich's personal dynamism and political savvy, could have played the cards that were dealt the House Republican leadership in the late 1980s and early 1990s as deftly as did the Georgian. But Cheney was not chancing it; he was tossing his hand on the table where he had played for a decade and looking to find a higher-stakes game.

Cheney's opportunity to gain a top-tier cabinet post came when père Bush's first choice for secretary of defense proved to be one of the most messed-up figures in American politics. Everyone knew that Texas senator John Tower, a long-standing friend of the Bush clan who had served as chair of the Senate Armed Services Committee during the Reagan years, enjoyed a drink, or five. The Bush team was not initially concerned; after all, the new president's son had quite a penchant for tequila. But it soon developed that, as Stephen Hess of the Brookings Institution put it, "the matter of John Tower was a disaster." Tower's troubles proved to be so severe that as reports of the senator's drinking, womanizing, and cozy relations with defense industry insiders surfaced, members of the Senate Armed Services Committee balked at the idea of handing so unhinged a character a role in making decisions about the deployment of nuclear weapons. When committee members rejected their former chair's nomination by a vote of 11–9, the *New York Times* observed "a growing impression in Washington" that the two-month-old administration was "adrift." Bush ordered his aides to come up with a reliable replacement with enough congressional connections to assure quick confirmation. The elder Bush's national security adviser, Brent Scowcroft, who had known Cheney from their days together in the Ford administration, asked the now familiar question "What about Dick?" The president quickly agreed to the suggestion of Cheney's name. There was no talk of Cheney's experience or vision with regard to the rapidly changing world—the Wyoming representative, who had never served in the military or on the House Armed Services Committee, was about as unconstructed a cold warrior as could be found in Congress. Rather, his selection was all about ending the embarrassment of having so significant a cabinet slot go unfilled for so long. As a member of Congress, it was presumed, Cheney would be approved quickly. The thinking was essentially correct. Senate minority leader Bob Dole, still stinging from the rejection of his friend Tower, grumbled, "This time it will be a confirmation, not an execution." Democrats on the Armed Services Committee fell into a pattern that would be repeated when Cheney named himself to the Republican ticket in 2000, misreading the nominee's moderate demeanor as an indication of his politics.

A *Washington Post* review of the Senate's reaction to Cheney's selection unintentionally summed up the Democratic penchant to underestimate his extremism with the line: "Sen. Charles S. Robb, D-Va., who voted against Tower, called Cheney 'an excellent choice' who is 'widely respected.' Saying he knows little about Cheney's views of foreign and defense policy, Robb added, 'He's so well-respected that unless there's a complete void in the area, confirmation should move rapidly.' " Cheney's confirmation hearing was an empty affair. In response to tepid questioning about his avoidance of the draft during the Vietnam War, Cheney simply lied and said that he "would have been happy to serve had I been called." Beyond that, the hearing was so devoid of substance that, as Donald Rumsfeld would recall years later, "in March of 1989, when [Cheney] appeared before this committee for his confirmation hearings, not one person uttered the word 'Iraq,' and within a year, he was preparing for U.S. war with Iraq." Typically, Rumsfeld was both wrong and right. Cheney was not preparing for war with Iraq a year after his confirmation hearing—the invasion of Kuwait did not occur until August 1990. But the neglect of the subject of Iraq, which was just finishing a horrific war with Iran, was emblematic of the casual character of the Cheney hearings. The committee had flexed its muscles in denying the president his first pick for secretary of defense, so they would give him his second choice.

By most accounts, Bush had relatively low expectations for Cheney. The president had appointed his friend James Baker as secretary of state and his friend Scowcroft as national security adviser. The important bases were covered, and all indications were that this new administration would be more prone to diplomacy than the defense buildups of the Reagan era. Bush suggested, in the press conference where he announced Cheney's selection, that he expected the new secretary of defense to focus on "the difficult challenges that he knows he faces of reforming the procurement process in the Pentagon." So it was that the man who was remembered for issuing memos about White House plumbing when he served as Ford's deputy chief of staff would now be worrying about those $600 toilet seats that the Department of Defense kept buying. Cheney did not mind; he took seriously any debate that involved the defense contractors with whom he had grown close as a member of Congress. In fact, he had a plan for making them a whole lot richer and himself a whole lot more powerful.

But first he had to make sure that no one got the wrong idea about the end of the cold war.

The new secretary of defense, who was described by the *Washington Post* as "the most hawkish" of Bush's close advisers, wanted to make it very clear to the American people and the world that the United States was not going to be getting out of the business of policing the planet. Even as Soviet influence crumbled in Eastern Europe and around the world, taking away the argument that for decades had been a given for U.S. military adventurism, Cheney appeared before a summer 1990 gathering of the World Affairs Council to declare, "I don't think the notion of a military threat to the interests of the United States was invented by the Communist Party of the Soviet Union, and I think it will be there long after the Communist Party of the Soviet Union no longer wields the interest that it has in the past."

Other members of the first Bush administration acknowledged that dangers were dwindling. "I'm running out of demons. I'm running out of villains," Joint Chiefs of Staff chairman Colin Powell told the *Army Times* in 1991. "I'm down to [Cuba's Fidel] Castro and [North Korea's] Kim II Sung." And leading figures in Congress, including some Republicans, proposed shifting hundreds of billions of dollars out of the Pentagon budget in order to fund human needs on the recession-ridden home front. But Cheney would have none of this peace dividend talk. He grumbled that even as "the breakup of the old order" was taking place, "we must hedge against the unexpected." Talk of a "peace dividend" was "irresponsible," Cheney claimed. Hedging against the unexpected was going to cost every bit as much as the cold war, and more. When Massachusetts senator Edward Kennedy and others of a liberal bent proposed slashing the defense budget to cover health care and education costs, Cheney griped about members of Congress who dared to claim that "there is some kind of big peace dividend here to be cashed in and to buy all the goodies everybody on Capitol Hill can think about buying."

In fact, there was a great big peace dividend to be had. Kennedy suggested that as much as $210 billion could be taken out of the Pentagon budget and used to pay for a national health care system and other needs. The Congressional Black Caucus proposed even deeper cuts in defense spending as part of a major redirection of national priorities. While exact figures might be debated, there was little question that the "peace dividend," properly spent, could have gone a long way toward ensuring domestic tranquillity and fostering the sort of international development that might have hindered the growth of terrorist networks during the 1990s. But Cheney, whose campaign accounts had been bloated with money from defense contractors such as Lockheed Corp., Martin Marietta Corp., McDonnel Douglas, TRW, and United Technologies, was not about to fritter away those relationships as he schemed to use his Pentagon posting as a platform from which to launch a 1996 presidential campaign that would require substantial special-interest funding. Cheney was determined to be the best friend the defense contractors ever had at the Pentagon—making himself, in the words of *New Yorker* writer Jane Mayer, "an architect and a beneficiary of the increasingly close relationship between the Department of Defense and an elite group of private military contractors." When cuts were required, Cheney made them at the human level, reducing the number of troops by 25 percent. But that did not mean the Department of Defense budgets were reduced by 25 percent; in fact, they held remarkably steady as Cheney shifted money from soldiers with names like Martinez and Cole to vendors with names like Bechtel and Halliburton. Cheney made it his mission to assure that military spending was maintained and that military contractors remained profitable. And he succeeded by putting a Department of Defense claim on every penny that might have gone to the peace dividend.

Cheney did not steer the United States away from the path of peace and international cooperation single-handedly. He worked as part of an administration that, while more inclined toward diplomacy and cooperation than the Reagan team that had preceded it, was never going to reform the budget process at home or reposition the United States in the world as thoroughly as would have the administration of a Democrat such as the technocratic Michael Dukakis or the visionary Gary Hart, who had made himself an expert on the Soviet Union and defense policy but proved to be less able when it came to avoiding the media missteps that crash campaigns for the presidency. Still, it would be a mistake to underestimate the impact of Cheney's selection as secretary of defense in 1989 and his guidance of the Pentagon in the four years that followed. Cheney's place at the center of defense policy making during that period assured that instead of distributing a "peace dividend," America would commit itself to implementing the vision Cheney laid out in a 1990 national defense strategy document that promised not only that "our military power will remain an essential underpinning of the global balance," but that the United States would "project power into areas where we have no permanent presence." As Chalmers Johnson observes in *The Sorrows of Empire* (2004), during Cheney's time as secretary of defense, "American ideologists managed to convince the public that the demise of the Soviet Union was evidence of a great American victory. This triumphalism, in turn, generated a subtle shift in the stance the United States had maintained throughout the Cold War. The United States no longer portrayed itself as a defensive power, seeking only to ensure its security and that of allied nations in the face of potential Soviet or Communist aggression. Without a superpower enemy, the first hints of the openly—proudly—imperial role it would take on in the new century emerged, as the Pentagon, rather than declaring victory and demobilizing, began to test the waters in a variety of new capacities, some of which would be expanded and some discarded in the years to come."

Once on the course that Cheney chose, Johnson observed, "The United States now assumed, slowly and by degrees, responsibility for humanitarian intervention, the spread of American-style 'market democracy' via globalization, open warfare against Latin American drug cartels and indigenous political reform movements, the quarantining of 'rogue states,' leadership of an endless 'war on terrorism,' and finally 'preventive' intervention against any potentially unfriendly power anywhere that threatened to possess the kinds of weapons of mass destruction the United States first developed and still wished to monopolize."

Did Cheney anticipate such dramatic developments? Probably not. After two decades of clawing his way ever closer to real power, Cheney had finally obtained it. But he had never worked up much of a vision regarding the place of the United States in the world, choosing instead to parrot the cold war fearmongering of conservative idealogues like John Ashbrook and Jesse Helms. In his early days at the Department of Defense, it appeared that his prime purpose was to maintain a military-industrial complex that served his own political interests and the business interests of his former and future campaign contributors and employers. To this end, the secretary of defense became a Cassandra, constantly conjuring up threats that had to be addressed. At times, Cheney seemed incoherent in his passion for maintaining the cold war. In the same speech, he would alternate between suggestions that the Soviets still posed a threat—long after other world leaders had come to recognize the break that Mikhail Gorbachev was making with the Soviet Union's past practices, Cheney remained in the camp of the most radical skeptics—and arguments that if Moscow was no longer the enemy it once was, then another foe would have to be found. It was essential, Cheney argued, for the United States to remove "any doubt in the minds of our allies around the world about our capacity and willingness to use force to keep our commitments, to protect our interests, to protect those of our friends and allies." To do this, Cheney argued, the United States had to get over its aversion to sending U.S. troops off to conquer countries that got out of line. When Secretary of State Baker suggested in 1989 that military action might be needed to depose Panamanian dictator Manuel Noriega, a petty thug who had recently stopped taking orders from his CIA and Defense Department paymasters, Cheney leapt at the opportunity. In doing so, he reversed the stance of his predecessor at the Pentagon, Reagan administration secretary of defense Frank Carlucci, who, with Admiral William Crowe, chairman of the Joint Chiefs of Staff, had rejected the idea that a full-scale military invasion of the Central American state was necessary or wise.

Cheney and the new chairman of the Joint Chiefs, a four-star general he had recruited for the post named Colin Powell, embraced the Panama invasion as an opportunity to flex military muscles that both men feared would go soft in the post–cold war era. "On Panama, Cheney and Powell were powerful collaborators, each in his own way contributing to a changing climate concerning America's willingness to send troops into military conflict," explains James Mann, who argues that "Panama was also the first military operation conducted with a post–Cold War rationale. When the United States invaded Grenada six years earlier, the stated purpose had been to prevent the spread of communism or Marxism, the same rationale that had been offered in other military operations since the Korean War. With Panama, the principle was different: America sent its troops for the purpose of restoring democracy and overthrowing a leader whose behavior was abhorrent. In this respect, Panama was a forerunner of the later American efforts against Saddam Hussein in Iraq."

Casual observers of history still suggest that the 1991 Persian Gulf War, which succeeded in its stated goal of ending the occupation of the corrupt but friendly oil-producing country of Kuwait by the corrupt but unfriendly oil-producing country of Iraq, was Cheney's great triumph as secretary of defense. But Cheney's role was, in fact, secondary. The first Persian Gulf War succeeded because of elaborate coalition building by President

Bush and Secretary of State James Baker and because of the restraint both men displayed when they and the general who was in charge on the ground, Norman Schwarzkopf, rejected proposals to "go all the way to Baghdad" after the Kuwaiti royal family was restored to power. Cheney had a role, of course. After the invasion of Kuwait in August 1990, President Bush declared that Iraq would either leave of its own accord or be forced to leave. To make the threat of force real, however, Bush needed to be able to move U.S. troops to Saudi Arabia's border with Kuwait. That required the approval of the Saudi royal family, which wholeheartedly objected to the precedent that was set by the displacement of the neighboring royals in Kuwait, but which chafed at the notion of allowing non-Muslim troops to use their country's soil as a base for military operations. With Paul Wolfowitz, his undersecretary of defense for policy, Cheney was dispatched to Saudi Arabia to convince King Fahd to accept the U.S. bases. Cheney was right when he said after the war, "It was a very important assignment. From a military standpoint if we could not get into Saudi Arabia it was going to be very hard for us to do anything militarily other than mount a naval blockade, for example." By the same token, in an administration packed with oil industry millionaires and oil industry millionaire wannabes, the Saudi Arabian assignment was a plum. Cheney got on well with the king and his minions, who would not learn until sometime later that the defense secretary and his aides had deceived them—displaying doctored satellite photos to suggest that an Iraqi invasion force had moved to the border in preparation for an invasion of Saudi Arabia. Not only did King Fahd approve the use of his country by the U.S. military, but he and other royals began to accept the secretary of defense into their inner circle. Cheney would soon find himself on the invite lists for royal weddings and other "family" events.

But the agreement forged by Wolfowitz and Cheney, men whose understanding of the religious and political dynamics of the Middle East were colored more by their determination to rid Israel of regional threats than by a real understanding of the issues that were in play in the Arab states, proved to be unpopular with many Saudis. One of them, a wealthy Muslim fundamentalist freshly returned from aiding the CIA-sponsored mujahideen forces that had defeated the Soviet occupation of Afghanistan, had told the Saudi royals that he wanted to build a religious army to remove the forces of the secularist Iraqi government from Kuwait. Osama bin Laden was furious that infidels had been handed the keys to the kingdom. He swore that he would wreak an awful vengeance upon the United States. As he built the al-Qaeda network that would be the vehicle for that vengeance, bin Laden regularly referenced the agreement by King Fahd to open Saudi Arabia to the Americans as a primary grievance. So it was that Cheney, who as secretary of defense prided himself on "getting the job done right" but whose limited background in global affairs invariably prevented him from doing so, assured the success of one war while unwittingly planting the seeds for another.

Aside from his dealings in Saudi Arabia, Cheney spent much of his time in the months before the first Persian Gulf War plotting a failed scheme to use the liberation of Kuwait as an excuse to depose Saddam Hussein. One of Cheney's aides, Henry Rowen, an academic from Stanford Business School who was moonlighting as the assistant secretary of defense for international security affairs, had become obsessed with the idea that the time was ripe for "regime change" in Iraq. He convinced Wolfowitz that as long as the U.S. military and its allies were in the region, it would be a good idea to take out Saddam Hussein, who among other things was seen as being particularly unfriendly to Israel. Rowen couldn't stop talking about Lawrence of Arabia and the Arab Legion and his certainty that it was possible to install a democracy in Iraq, and Cheney couldn't stop listening.

Along with Wolfowitz, Cheney liked Rowen's bold thinking. In an interview a decade later, Rowen recalled Cheney telling him to "set up a team [to explore the idea], and don't tell Powell or anybody else." Suddenly, as James Mann has observed, "the defense secretary was quietly campaigning for a war plan different from the one submitted by the chairman of the Joint Chiefs of Staff."

Famously, Cheney told Colin Powell during this time to "stick to military matters." But it was actually Cheney and his aides who were expanding their job descriptions. Cheney's secret team came up with Operation Scorpion, an elaborate plan that involved sending U.S. troops to remote regions west of Baghdad, from which they could, presumably, threaten Saddam. Schwarzkopf got wind of the scheme and pointed out that it would be impossible to supply troops who were dispatched to the distant deserts of western Iraq. Bush and Baker, who recognized the diplomatic disaster that the plan to depose an Arab leader would create, backed the general, and Operation Scorpion was quickly consigned to the dustbin of history—although Cheney and Wolfowitz would continue to entertain fantasies about "decapitating" Saddam and imposing "regime change." The Operation Scorpion plot raised real questions about Cheney's capacity to contribute to the war effort. Schwarzkopf would later express his frustration with Cheney's Operation Scorpion scheming, observing, "I wondered whether Cheney had succumbed to the phenomenon I'd observed among some secretaries of the army. Put a civilian in charge of professional military men and before long he's no longer satisfied with setting policy but wants to out-general the generals."

Duly chastened, Cheney, whom the *Washington Post* took to referring to as "the desk-chair warrior," faded from the forefront of the Iraq effort. He was still part of the team, still rebuking and even firing aides who responded to questions from the media, and still offering bad advice, such as his counsel that Bush did not need congressional approval to wage the war. But, as Phil McCombs noted in an April 1991 profile for the *Washington Post,* "When the war was over, America seemingly stood atop golden hours. Bush basked in his 91 percent approval rating, Powell was being touted for—at least—vice president, and two publishing houses were scheduling instant books on Stormin' Norman Schwarzkopf, the growling, tenderhearted commander of Desert Storm. But where was Cheney?" The article recounted the surprise on the part of key players in Washington when they heard a reporter was interested in profiling Cheney: " 'Wow, Cheney?' exclaimed an aide to former defense secretary Frank Carlucci, who with Cheney, [Ken] Adelman and Donald Rumsfeld had been a bright young Nixonaut at the Office of Economic Opportunity, where they set about dismantling the poverty program. 'We've had 500 requests for interviews about Powell. This is the first one for Cheney.' "

Like so many of his attempts to put his imprint on an important endeavor, from the Ford reelection campaign to the second Bush administration's energy policy, Cheney had screwed up. But the war was polling well. Besides, Washington is a town that pays greater rewards for loyalty and discretion than it ever does for vision or success. So Cheney, who never ceases to survey whatever political landscape in which he finds himself for advantage and opportunity, set to work spinning himself as the real winner of the Gulf War. And for the most part, he succeeded. Soon, only a few insiders would remember that the secretary of defense had been caught peddling unworkable and dangerous schemes behind the scenes. In an increasingly stenographic media, Cheney knew he could and would be portrayed in the manner he preferred: as the calm, technocratic manager who had achieved his mission with a minimum of fuss. In no time, major newspapers such as the *Los Angeles Times* were describing Cheney as "presidential timber."

Cheney was certainly thinking presidential. But in the short term, the defense secretary knew he needed to get back to the demanding work that had consumed him before Saddam Hussein's troops entered Kuwait City: pocketing the peace dividend. In pursuit of this broader and bolder goal, the Gulf War was merely a footnote to the central mission of maintaining a military-industrial complex that Cheney saw as a source of both power and the campaign money that might make a presidential bid possible. After the war was done, Cheney set out to declare a different kind of victory from what others saw. Instead of recognizing the relative ease with which U.S. forces prevailed in Kuwait and beyond as evidence that the United States was well-enough prepared to meet any challenge, Cheney began talking about the need to make sure the United States would "have the capacity to send force to defend our interests to wherever they're threatened." While he did not suggest in so many words that the

"Big-Time" Media Critic

George W. Bush does not read newspapers. Nor does he watch much television news. He says that he relies on his aides to provide him with the information he needs.

And, of course, Dick Cheney is the adviser-in-chief.

Thus, just as when Cheney "let" Bush determine that the best Republican running mate would be, er, Dick Cheney, so the vice president fills in the considerable gaps in the president-in-name-only's knowledge base with an eye toward achieving his own ends. Cheney is no fool in this regard. Recognizing that he is an unpopular figure within the administration and in the country at large, he goes to great pains to foster the fantasy that Bush is regularly handed a full pallet of proposals—from which the president, presumably, picks the plan that matches his mood.

But the pallet never offers real choices, as should be obvious by now. Former Treasury secretary Paul O'Neill and other refugees from the Bush White House have noted in agonizing detail that this is not a White House that entertains a lively intellectual discourse. In part, this is because Cheney plays the role of ideological commissar, constricting and manipulating the flow of information and ideas to conform to his political and personal purposes.

But it is important to remember that while Cheney does read newspapers and magazines, listen to the radio, and watch television news programs, he does so with a bias. He likes his media pliant and unquestioning. For instance, the vice president recently told a gathering of journalists that in the aftermath of the September 11, 2001, terrorist attacks on the World Trade Center and the Pentagon, when television anchors started sporting flag pins and the quality of reporting was so inept that most Americans actually thought Saddam Hussein's Iraq was somehow linked to the violence, "American journalism produced some of its finest work ever."

Dick Cheney does not have a taste for media that might challenge his preconceived notions. And he has never approved of reporters who believe the White House has a duty to communicate critical information to the American people. Cheney is not joking when he says, "It's easy to complain about the press—I've been doing it for a good part of my career."

A militant when it comes to White House secrecy, Cheney has a long history of punishing aides who cooperate with reporters—before the 1991 Persian Gulf War, then secretary of defense Cheney fired air force chief of staff General Michael J. Dugan for discussing general war planning with the *Washington Post*.

But, while Cheney can be rough on his subordinates, he is even rougher with the rare journalist who seeks to be anything more than a stenographer for the White House.

Cheney summed up his attitude when during a campaign stop in Naperville, Illinois, in 2000, non-newspaper reader Bush noted the presence of one of the few reporters he actually knew by name.

"There's Adam Clymer—major-league asshole—from the *New York Times*," grumbled Bush.

"Yeah, big-time," said Cheney.

Clymer was not the first journalist to end up on Cheney's "big-time" asshole list. A quarter-century before the 2000 incident, when Cheney was serving as the White House chief of staff in Gerald Ford's administration, he organized a West Wing discussion about how to launch a criminal investigation of journalist Seymour Hersh—and the *New York Times,* for which Hersh was writing then. In May 1975, Hersh had written an article exposing the fact that U.S. Navy submarines had intercepted high-level Soviet military communiqués by tapping into underwater telecommunications cables. Only after learning that the Soviets were not surprised by the spying—presumably, they expected it—did Cheney back off from the discussion of how best to go after one of the nation's most respected investigative journalists.

(Cheney's concern for protecting intelligence gathering operations is somewhat episodic. While he coordinated the debate about how to go after Hersh in the 1970s, he convened no such discussion in 2003, when concerns were raised about the prospect that Cheney or a member of his staff had "outed" CIA agent Valerie Plame, the wife of former ambassador Joe Wilson, who had exposed the dubious use of intelligence by a White House that was bent on making a "case" for war with Iraq.)

Hersh and Clymer need not feel particularly insulted. Throughout his career, Cheney has generally viewed journalists as the enemy. In April 2003, shortly after the invasion of Iraq, the vice president reacted to reports that U.S. troops had killed three journalists on the same day, after firing into the Baghdad office of the al-Jazeera network and the Palestine Hotel, where many international reporters were staying. Cheney casually announced that this was "the sort of thing that happens in warfare." Cheney declared that "you'd have to be an idiot to believe that [the attacks were intentional]." But around the world, leaders of journalist organizations, diplomats, and prominent political figures expressed precisely that concern.

Cheney's disregard for the fourth estate is not universal, however. He has always had favorite journalists, some of whom are able choniclers of the conservative cause (such as the *Washington Post*'s Lou Cannon) but most of whom are the stenographers to power who peddle White House talking points as "news."

Cheney divides the journalistic community into two camps: "big-time" assholes versus employees of Australian-born media mogul Rupert Murdoch's far-flung empire. Murdoch's ideological organ, the *Weekly Standard,* may not have many readers outside the narrow circle of neoconservatives who still think the war in Iraq was a good idea. But it enjoys high circulation inside the White House. Editor William Kristol likes to suggest that the journal of uninspired imperialism has "induced" Cheney and others to embrace his publication's faith that America is ideally suited to fill the void left by the decline of the British Empire. Editors always like to imagine influences that may or may not exist. But, in this case, Kristol can point to some mighty solid evidence of Cheney's devotion to the *Standard* vision. As he notes, "Dick Cheney does send someone to pick up 30 copies of the magazine every Monday."

Cheney is no elitist when it comes to Murdoch's products, however. A big viewer of the talk shows that clog cable channels with nightly conservative diatribes, Cheney delights in the programming on Murdoch's Fox News Channel. Indeed, he's a regular Fox aficionado.

Cheney, who in March 2004 proudly noted that "my last full-blown press conference was when I was secretary of defense in April of 1991," may not have much time for most media. But Murdoch's Fox News Channel, the court reporter of the Bush administration, can always count on an interview, a leak, or, as happened in April 2004, an official endorsement from the vice president. "What I do is try to focus on the elements of the press that I think do an effective job and try to be accurate in their portrayal of events," Cheney told Republican activists who were griping about the media. "For example, I end up spending a lot of time watching Fox News, because they're more accurate in my experience, in those events that I'm personally involved in, than many of the other outlets."

So let's be clear about where the White House gets its "independent confirmation" of the news of the day. Bush does not read newspapers or watch the news, while Cheney reads the *Weekly Standard* and watches Fox. Come to think of it, maybe Cheney isn't really in charge. Maybe Rupert Murdoch is the boss.

United States should have gone on to Baghdad to implement the "regime change" imagined by the drafters of Operation Scorpion, he did begin to argue that the Pentagon needed to maintain the ability to complete such projects in the future. Despite the success of the coalition cobbled together by Bush and Baker, and despite the support of the United Nations, Cheney envisioned a far more unilateral future. The United States needed a plan for making war whenever it wanted, wherever it wanted, with or without the approval of the rest of the world.

To this end, Cheney manipulated Congress to limit proposed cuts in Pentagon budgets. To be sure, hits were taken here and there. But Cheney assured that they were only flesh wounds. "After the fall of the Berlin Wall," observed *Washington Post* writer Dana Milbank, "Cheney, as defense secretary, practiced a form of gamesmanship with Congress. Facing certain cuts, Cheney decided to put three items on the chopping block rather than let Congress do the cutting for him. He offered up cuts in the National Guard, base closures, and the V-22 Osprey [a widely discredited helicopter project], knowing full well that Congress would balk. Congress 'won' the battle by refusing to make many of the cuts, but Cheney therefore had leverage in protecting his priorities." Those priorities were not surprising for a man who had worked so hard to avoid wearing the uniform of his country: Cheney was willing to cut back when it came to caring for the troops, but he was quick to object when defense contractors faced the budget ax. And considering the times, he was stunningly successful. Though the Cheney team lost "some" battles, recalled David Gribben, who served as the Pentagon's legislative director, "we got 90 percent of what we wanted."

Gribben underestimated their success. Any short-term cuts

that were forced upon Cheney's Pentagon were soon offset by a scheme that would, in time, erase even the memory of the proposed peace dividend of the early 1990s.

With Cheney prodding them, Wolfowitz and his top aide, I. Lewis "Scooter" Libby, began working with another member of their team, Zalmay Khalilzad, to use the biennial process of plotting military strategy and setting Department of Defense budget priorities, the Defense Planning Guidance, as a vehicle for promoting a radical interpretation of the proper role of the United States in the post–cold war world. Working in secret, they produced a 1992 Defense Planning Guidance document that read like an imperialist manifesto from one of the old European colonial powers. While others spoke of a new internationalism, Cheney's crew imagined America as the ultimate military superpower. Their United States would not merely respond to threats from abroad, it would "prevent any hostile power from dominating a region whose resources would, under consolidated control, be sufficient to generate global power." The document, which was slipped to a *New York Times* reporter in 1992, was stunningly blunt in describing the resources over which the new America would go to war: "In the Middle East and Southwest Asia, our overall objective is to remain the predominant outside power in the region and preserve U.S. and western access to the region's oil."

The leaking of the Defense Planning Guidance document caused a furor, especially when newspaper headlines screamed, KEEPING THE U.S. FIRST: PENTAGON WOULD PRECLUDE A RIVAL SUPERPOWER. The giddiness of the days and weeks immediately following the liberation of Kuwait had faded, and it looked as if President Bush might face a tougher than expected reelection challenge from a brash southern governor named Bill Clinton. Bush and Baker did not want to spend the year arguing about empire and imperialism. On May 24, 1992, a *New York Times* headline read, PENTAGON DROPS GOAL OF BLOCKING NEW SU-PERPOWERS. This time, however, the *Times* was not presenting all the news that was fit to print. Cheney refused to abandon the project. Indeed, he was more enthusiastic than ever about it. Even as the controversy caused by the leak of the document raged, Khalilzad (who by 2004 would be serving as U.S. ambassador to Afghanistan) said Cheney hailed the draft of the Defense Planning Guidance, telling his aide, "You've discovered a new rationale for our role in the world."

Wolfowitz's lieutenant, Scooter Libby, set out to rewrite the Defense Planning Guidance with gentler language but no less menacing intent. According to James Mann, Libby was not out to soften the statement. Mann explained that Cheney's aide believed "the main point shouldn't be to block rival powers, but rather for the United States to become so militarily strong, so overwhelming, that no country would dream of ever becoming a rival." The purpose was to assure that "the United States would be the world's lone superpower not just today or ten years from now, but permanently."

The "Defense Strategy for the 1990s" document that appeared above Cheney's name in the last days of the Bush presidency was, on the surface, more palatable to official Washington. But it remained a unilateralist manifesto that again and again spoke of the need to "shape the future" and "shape the world." Libby's contribution was to suggest, rather unconvincingly, that the United States would be willing to work with "democratic and like-minded nations." But the document constantly questioned the reliability and value of multinational initiatives, while suggesting that "U.S. leadership may be crucial to catalyze such action. . . . We will, therefore, not ignore the need to be prepared to protect our critical interests and honor our commitments with only limited additional help, or even alone, if necessary," it declared. "A future President will need options allowing him to lead and, where the international reaction proves sluggish or inadequate, to act independently to protect our critical interests."

A decade later, as the most powerful vice president in American history, Dick Cheney would identify those critical interests as lying in the deserts of Iraq, where he had once hoped to dispatch American troops as part of Operation Scorpion. As 2002 turned to 2003, international reaction was not merely sluggish and inadequate, it was passionately opposed to the "regime change" mission that Cheney proposed. But by then, there was no one powerful enough to say no to Cheney's madness. Secretary of State Colin Powell questioned the dossier that Scooter Libby and other Cheney aides threw together to make the "case" that Iraq possessed weapons of mass destruction, but there was no higher authority to whom he could appeal. Cheney, the de facto commander in chief, had forged a new rationale for the U.S. role in the world, and he was damn well going to use it.

Cheney believed that forging this new rationale for U.S. military intervention and adventurism abroad was the great achievement of the first Bush administration, just as he believed turning that rationale into the reality of war with Iraq would be the greatest achievement of the second Bush administration. When they had wandered in the political wilderness of the Clinton years, Cheney and his aides had given their passion a name: the Project for the New American Century. It was an appropriate title, for their experiment had determined the direction not just of foreign policy, but also of domestic policy within the American homeland. To create the combination of military might and political will that would enable the United States to act as it pleased abroad, Cheney and his conservative allies in the executive and legislative branches of successive governments had robbed the public treasury of the funds needed to maintain the domestic social programs they so despised. Defense spending, which thanks to Cheney's interventions as secretary of defense never took the hits that had been anticipated during the first Bush administration, rose during the second Bush administration to the highest level in the history of the United States. Today, the United States spends more on armaments, armies, and privatized defense contracts than any nation in the history of the world. And no one in a position of authority talks anymore about using a peace dividend to pay for "goodies" such as health care and education. How could they? The peace dividend was cashed in a long time ago, by Dick Cheney.

CHAPTER 6

CEO OF THE U.S.A.

I tell you that the government had absolutely nothing to do with it.
> —Dick Cheney, 2000, rejecting claims that he used his
> government contacts to enrich Halliburton and himself

Under the guidance of Dick Cheney, a get-the-government-out-of-my-face conservative, Halliburton Company over the past five years has emerged as a corporate welfare hog, benefiting from at least $3.8 billion in federal contracts and taxpayer-insured loans.
> —Center for Public Integrity, 2000, from the report
> *Cheney Led Halliburton to Feast at Federal Trough*

He doesn't see the difference between public and private interest.
> —Colonel Sam Gardiner (USAF, ret.), 2004, on
> Dick Cheney's inability to recognize conflicts

In the waning days of George Herbert Walker Bush's presidency, Secretary of Defense Dick Cheney busied himself with a bold new project. He wrongly presumed that the president who had achieved 91 percent approval ratings during the Persian Gulf War could not be beaten by Bill Clinton, the Democrat whom Republicans derided as "the unknown governor of a state no

DAVID VALDEZ/WHITE HOUSE/TIME LIFE PICTURES/GETTY IMAGES

War profiteers: Before leaving the administration of Bush I, Cheney gave Halliburton subsidiary Brown & Root Services almost $9 million to study whether private firms like, er, Brown & Root should take over logistical support for U.S. military operations. After a failed bid for the presidency, Cheney became Halliburton's CEO, eventually pocketing $44 million in private sector dollars. (1991)

one can find on a map." Cheney's political instincts again proved to be deeply flawed.

But his instincts regarding the prospects for remaking the nation's military-industrial complex as a more integrated, more powerful, yet dramatically less accountable entity were right on target. During the early 1990s, the political catchphrase of the moment was "reinventing government." With a recession eating away at revenues and conservatives honing their "no-new-taxes" pitches, every agency in Washington was looking for ways to economize while increasing efficiency. Cheney came up with the ultimate "reinventing government" scheme. He would privatize the military's logistical operations. To Cheney's view, this was a win-win scenario. At a time when the military was under pressure to downsize, privatization of everything from digging latrines to running mess halls would allow the Department of Defense to cut hundreds of thousands of jobs—eliminating the need to provide not just pay, but housing, education, health care, and retirement benefits for career military men and women and their families. At the same time, it would guide billions of additional dollars into the accounts of defense contractors who would form a force powerful enough to guarantee that defense budgets would never again face the threat of a peace dividend. Unlike soldiers and sailors, defense contractors were in a position to make hefty campaign contributions and send legions of lobbyists to Capitol Hill, meaning that the Pentagon would have critical support in the budget fights that were sure to come.

For Cheney, who assumed that he would be serving as secretary of defense in a second Bush administration, while preparing to challenge the hapless Dan Quayle for the 1996 Republican presidential nomination, the appeal of his privatization scheme was obvious: defense contractors would be pleased and surely grateful when it came time to open campaign contribution checkbooks. To sell the notion that the military ought to barter off so many of its responsibilities would not be easy, however. There were generals who worried about upsetting the command structure, members of Congress who grumbled about creating new arenas for procurement abuses, and public-interest groups that saw the potential for governmental and political corruption on a monumental scale.

Cheney knew he would have to make the case for radically changing the way in which the military did business. To do this, he would need a serious study, a document to make the argument that privatization would not just save money, but make America more secure. But who could produce such a study? What independent, disinterested, above reproach groups could be counted on to fully and fairly assess so critical a question? The Pentagon's own research and analysis teams? No. The Congressional Budget Office? No. Perhaps a think tank with a long history of monitoring military expenditures and programs? No. Cheney had a better idea. How about Halliburton?

That's right. In 1992, Dick Cheney's Department of Defense paid Halliburton's construction subsidiary, Brown & Root Services, $3.9 million to analyze the strengths and weaknesses of the argument for permitting private firms, such as, er, Brown & Root, to provide logistical support for U.S. military operations in hot spots around the world. Cheney and his aides were apparently impressed by the classified report they received from Brown & Root. Before the year was out, they allocated another $5 million to have the firm beef up its study. "In effect," explained the *New Yorker*'s Jane Mayer in a perceptive study of the vice president and his former employer, "the company was being asked to create its own market." Within a decade, that "market" would be worth more than $150 billion a year to defense contractors. But the first critical step in opening it for business was taken almost without notice. Even as the Brown & Root studies were being reviewed and updated, Cheney's Department of Defense was moving to implement their recommendations. In the months before they turned over the Pentagon to the incoming Clinton administration, the Cheney-led Pentagon performed a sweeping reinvention of government. In August 1992, Brown & Root was quietly awarded a logistics contract from the U.S. Army Corps of Engineers that would permit it to work alongside soldiers in Haiti, Somalia, the Balkans, and everywhere else the military came ashore.

In those recessionary days, when many construction firms were struggling to keep afloat, it appeared that business was going to be very good for Brown & Root and, by extension, Halliburton. For its work in the Balkans alone, the firm's contract with the Department of Defense yielded $2.2 billion in payments from the U.S. Treasury during the mid-1990s. Even the disastrous U.S. experience in Somalia, which formed the basis for the film *Black Hawk Down,* was good for Halliburton. The company pocketed $109 million for providing troop support and preparing the bodies of the dead for burial. With the Pentagon pipeline open, Halliburton went from strength to strength.

Fortune shined, as well, on Dick Cheney, who in short order would move from dispensing Department of Defense checks to collecting them as Halliburton's chairman and chief executive officer.

Dick Cheney's official association with Halliburton lasted

just five years, from 1995 to 2000. Yet it would make him a very rich, and very well-connected, man. He would begin to move in the circles of the high-flying corporate elites who were the demigods of the decade—men like Enron's Ken Lay. And while Cheney collected $44 million in private sector dollars, he would, by virtue of his position at the helm of one of the nation's primary defense contractors, remain the pivotal player that he thought he should be in debates about the direction of U.S. foreign policy.

Indeed, as the privatization process that Cheney set in motion during those last days at the Pentagon began to speed up, he was uniquely positioned to engage in the most critical dialogues regarding the nation's future without having to consign himself to the indignity of a government paycheck.

"Privatization is a way of going around Congress and not telling the public," Colonel Bruce Grant explained in a 2002 *Foreign Policy in Focus* special report that reviewed "oversight issues" arising from the increasing use of private firms to perform work that only a few years earlier had been the responsibility of military men and women. "Foreign policy is made by default by private military consultants motivated by bottom-line profits," Grant complained. While analysts such as Peter Singer of the Brookings Institution worried that "we're turning the lifeblood of our defense over to the marketplace," insiders like Cheney wisely positioned themselves in that marketplace—knowing that they could wield a new kind of not quite public, not quite private power. Cheney understood this reality better than just about anyone in the rapidly reshaping military-industrial complex. Yet the CEO gig at Halliburton was never Cheney's endgame. He was just collecting a debt when, as had happened before, his best-laid plans went awry. As lucrative as it might have been, Cheney's tenure at Halliburton was merely a detour for a man who still entertained dreams of attaining the one CEO title that trumped all others: commander in chief.

When the voters of the United States handed George Herbert Walker Bush and Dick Cheney their pink slips in 1992, Bush knew his long career in government service had come to a close. But Cheney, ever prone to delusions of political grandeur, did not want to occupy just any executive office. He wanted the Oval Office. The elder Bush was finished, and the family had not yet fully groomed the former president's one able son, Jeb, for a run to reclaim the White House. There was an opening for an establishment candidate who could credibly appeal to the conservative cadres that had come to dominate the Republican Party's grass roots. Plenty of candidates were positioning themselves to fill that opening, but Cheney thought he was on the inside track. After all, with his secretary of defense duties behind him, he had completed a classic Republican résumé—White House chief of staff, leader in Congress, key player in a war cabinet—and any memories of his associations with Gerald Ford and the moderate wing of the Republican Party had been papered over by a voting record every bit as draconian as those of the GOP's darkest players. Cheney was never all that good at politics, but after a quarter century of doing everything from holding the button bag for Warren Knowles to mismanaging Gerald Ford's reelection campaign to winning his own races for the House in Wyoming, he had come to understand at least some of the basics of mounting a presidential campaign.

Step one was to find a platform from which to make lofty pronouncements about his own merits and the demerits of

President Clinton. The always politically pliable American Enterprise Institute, a corporation-funded "think tank" that provides paychecks and office space to out-of-work politicos and whacked-out ideologues such as rejected Supreme Court nominee Robert Bork and *The Bell Curve* author Charles Murray, gave both Dick and Lynne Cheney fellowships. Lynne wrote a book titled *Telling the Truth,* while Dick set out to do the opposite.

The Cheney for President campaign never really amounted to anything more than a pile of speeches and campaign fundraising receipts. The rationale for his candidacy was "obvious" to Cheney. "Obviously, it's something I'll take a look at," he told Larry King during a "Hey, I'm available" appearance on CNN a few days after Clinton was inaugurated in January 1993. "Obviously, I've worked for three presidents and watched two others up close, and so it is an idea that has occurred to me."

It did not seem so obvious to anyone else, however. Cheney toured around the country for the better part of two years, visiting forty states, delivering Lincoln Day dinner addresses, and accepting second billing to local pols at bean feeds. There was some quiet questioning among party bosses about whether the Republicans really wanted to challenge the still relatively young and virile Bill Clinton with a fellow who had suffered three heart attacks in eighteen years and had the scars from quadruple bypass surgery. Still, Cheney raised enough money to keep the show on the road—collecting $1 million, including checks from executives of corporations that had benefited from his tenure as secretary of defense, such as Halliburton, Bechtel, and Science Applications International Corp. (All three firms would manage to gain huge contracts to rebuild Iraq during the second Bush administration, in which Cheney would emerge as a considerably more influential figure than he had been in the first.) But the big money never really came Cheney's way, and grassroots Republicans dismissed him as a boring Alexander Haig. The hard-liners gave Cheney reasonably high marks for Clinton bashing and general cruelty (he dismissed concerns about access to health care as "a manufactured crisis" and declared that the real problem in America was "a criminal justice system that hands out lengthy prison sentences to law-enforcement officers who use excessive force"). For the most part, however, the response to Cheney's campaign was a yawn. As had been the complaint since his first congressional run, this candidate could go into a room of enthusiasts and turn them into skeptics. Instead of a stump speech, he delivered a lecture: "I am concerned that as a nation we have relegated foreign and defense policy to last place on the public agenda—at the precise moment when the world is most in need of American leadership," he grumbled in a December 1993 address, before launching into a lengthy dissertation on the recent developments in Moldova and Armenia. Cheney's campaign had a listless, almost whimsical character. "I drove eight thousand miles across the country, by myself, deciding on the spur of the moment which route to follow, stopping at the McDonald's hamburger joints and the truck stops, hitting the back roads as well as the interstates. Along the way I made a few speeches . . . ," he would recall after it was done. At the same time, Bob Dole was jetting across the country, winning the endorsements of Republican governors. Cheney couldn't even get the new governor of Texas, George W. Bush, interested in his candidacy. And early in 1995, the disappointed contender folded the Cheney for President campaign and went fly-fishing in New Brunswick, Canada.

As it happencd, Cheney's fishing partners were a group of corporate bigwigs who were concerned about the coming transition at Halliburton, a firm that was in the process of a management shuffle. "After Cheney had said good night, the others began talking about Halliburton's need for a new CEO. Why not Dick? He had virtually no business experience, but he had valuable relationships with very powerful people," explained a re-creation of events published in the *New Yorker.* Cheney's lack of business experience was not a problem, as he wasn't exactly going into business. Rather, his job would be to build upon the relationships that had begun to develop when he was secretary of defense. If anybody knew how to get more Defense Department dollars into Halliburton's accounts, it was the man who used to run the Defense Department. From Halliburton's standpoint, this looked like a marriage made in heaven, and from Cheney's standpoint, this looked like a job that would put him close to the center of the military-industrial complex he had worked so hard to preserve—and to the power that position would afford him. Of course, these were not the calculations that were described to the public when Cheney's selection was announced at an August 1995 press conference in Dallas. The official line was that Cheney was getting out of politics. "When I made the decision earlier this year not to run for president, not to seek the White House," the newly minted CEO explained, "that really was a decision to wrap up my political career and move on to other things."

Cheney was lying.

He was joining Halliburton to help the firm close the sorts of deals he had set up as secretary of defense. In an unguarded moment, the *Washington Post* revealed at least part of the plan, reporting, "As secretary of defense during the Persian Gulf War, Cheney made international contacts which Halliburton executives hoped would propel the company to the industry's fore." There was never any mystery about why Cheney was hired. His job was to use his connections to help Halliburton make a whole lot of money very, very quickly, and Halliburton would, in turn, help Dick Cheney make a whole lot of money very, very quickly. This was not going to be a permanent relationship. When the Republican exile from the White House was done, the new CEO fully expected to return to Washington. Anyone who thought he had given up the dream of running the United States did not know Dick Cheney.

The moneymaking side of the equation came together pretty much as expected. Cheney proved, literally, to be worth his weight in gold. Halliburton's revenues doubled during the time that he served as CEO, to more than $15 billion annually. And the corporation, which had been slogging along in the "second tier" of the energy industry, grew to be the world's largest oil and gas services company. Cheney got a good deal of the credit for that growth; a CNN *Money* report pubished shortly after he placed himself on the 2000 Republican ticket was headlined CHENEY GETS "A" AS CEO. But don't get the impression that Cheney was some kind of business genius. The one major merger Cheney oversaw, the acquisition in 1998 of Dresser Industries, Halliburton's chief rival, doubled the size of the company. That looked great on the surface, but the fine print was a mess. The official spin has it that Cheney is a meticulous detail man who reads through mounds of briefing papers and never stops asking questions. In fact, he is famously lax when it comes to research and has a history of deciding what he wants to do and then forcing the facts to conform to his whims about everything from politics to business to imaginary connections between Osama bin Laden and Saddam Hussein. The acquisition of Dresser Industries was a classic example of Cheney's "decide first, analyze later" approach. The Halliburton CEO and his lieutenants were so enthusiastic about doubling the size of the company that they failed to examine Dresser's liabilities, which included a stack of lawsuits against a Dresser subsidiary, Harbison-Walker Refractories, which stood accused of exposing workers at its Pittsburgh factory to asbestos. "I never understood why they did that," Dallas attorney John Wall said of Halliburton's acquisition of its troubled competitor. "They overpaid for Dresser, and all they did was buy a bunch of liabilities." When the claims were pursued against Halliburton, according to the *New Yorker*'s Jane Mayer, they "proved so ruinous that several Halliburton divisions later filed for bankruptcy protection. The asbestos settlements devastated the company's stock price, which fell by eighty percent in just over a year." For all the hoopla about how Cheney built up Halliburton, after the lawsuit time bomb finally exploded, the company's stock was selling for $3 less a share than at the time when Cheney came on as CEO. As former secretary of state Lawrence Eagleburger, a Halliburton board member, put it, "Somebody slipped up somewhere in the due diligence." Eagleburger's not blaming his friend Cheney, mind you, he's just saying, "Somebody should have caught it."

Okay, so mergers weren't Cheney's thing. Not a problem. Despite his CEO title, Cheney wasn't really expected to worry about traditional business concerns like whether an acquisition will prove to be an asset or a liability. Rather, as former Halliburton CEO Tom Cruikshank, the man who recuited Cheney, told *USA Today* in 2002, "We had people who could handle the details. That's not what we wanted him for. What we needed was someone . . . who could help in obtaining business, generating revenues. Dick had stature and access to customers around the world for us. That was one of the attractions." Translation: Cheney was hired as a rainmaker. And Halliburton needed one. Older Halliburton hands recalled the "glory days" of the 1960s, when Texan Lyndon Johnson—whose rise in politics had, according to local lore, been funded by envelopes full of cash from Brown & Root founders George and Herman Brown—steered 85 percent of the lucrative contracts for servicing his Southeast Asian war making to the good old boys at Brown & Root. (Soldiers on the ground in Vietnam referred to the firm as "Burn & Loot.") But other companies, such as Bechtel, had elbowed their way up to the federal trough, and Halliburton had fallen to seventy-third place on the Department of Defense list of top contractors. With his privatization scheming, Cheney had opened up a new spigot of Pentagon cash, and his friends in Dallas wanted him to steer the money into Halliburton's bank accounts. At the same time, they wanted the man who had built up relationships with everyone from the Saudi royal family to the leaders of the Chinese Communist Party to sell officials in other countries on the notion that doing business with Halliburton was just like doing business with the United States of America.

With respect to the firm's accumulation of contracts and other benefits from the U.S. government, the title of a study produced by the Center for Public Integrity well summed up the contribution that the former secretary of defense made to his new employer: *Cheney Led Halliburton to Feast at Federal Trough.*

The report detailed how, "under the guidance of Dick Cheney, a get-the-government-out-of-my-face conservative, Halliburton Company over the past five years has emerged as a corporate welfare hog, benefiting from at least $3.8 billion in federal contracts and taxpayer-insured loans."

To be fair to Cheney, while he was a liberal about feasting from the trough, he remained true to his conservative principles when it came to replenishing it. During Cheney's time as CEO, Halliburton arranged for itself to essentially stop paying U.S. taxes. While the company was chipping in as much as $302 million in federal taxes during the early days of Cheney's time as CEO, by 1999 the highly profitable firm actually collected a rebate of $85 million from the feds. How'd he do it? By moving corporate assets "offshore" to "tax havens" that were friendly to corporations hiding from IRS agents. Between 1995 and 1999, the number of Halliburton subsidiaries registered outside the United States multiplied from nine to forty-four. A CBS *60 Minutes* investigation in 2004 revealed that a number of these Halliburton satellites were little more than post office boxes and sheds.

But Halliburton was hardly the only company that avoided paying taxes in the late 1990s, just as it was hardly the only company that employed Enron-style accounting tricks to fool Wall Street and its own investors. What made Halliburton unique, what made it the hub of the military-industrial complex, and what would eventually make its name synonymous with the most egregious corporate corruption, was a rainmaking, tree-shaking, money-grubbing sugar daddy named Dick Cheney, who proved that when you write the rules, it really isn't all that hard to win.

Here's how Cheney turned Halliburton into the Franken-stein's monster of public-private partnerships:

1. At the head of a team of former government employees, which included veteran Cheney aide and former Department of Defense chief of staff Dave Gribben, who became Halliburton's man on the ground in Washington, Cheney launched an aggressive campaign to make Brown & Root the go-to contractor for the U.S. military. With Congress controlled by Republican advocates for privatization like House Speaker Newt Gingrich, who also happened to be a friend and former colleague of Cheney's, and with the media cutting back on coverage of government agencies and "boring" stories about bids and contracts, Cheney and his team operated with little or no scrutiny. Unbothered by questions about the conflicts of interest that necessarily arise when someone sets up a government privatization program and then moves to the private firm that is poised to profit from that program, Cheney and his merry band of corporate welfare warriors essentially set up shop in the Pentagon. As the U.S. Army, in particular, began to privatize more and more essential services, Halliburton's team reported for duty. During the five years before Cheney took charge of Halliburton, the firm collected $1.2 billion in federal government largesse. During the five years that Cheney was in charge, Halliburton grabbed $2.3 billion out of the U.S. Treasury. And the gravy train was just beginning to roll.

The news that Cheney had selected himself to be vice president was greeted with glee in Halliburton's headquarters. Sure, they would miss the gruff guy, but as a Center for Public Integrity report noted in 2000, "Wall Street analysts praise Cheney's stewardship of the company and attribute his ability to attract government contracts and grants to his high-level access to the corridors of power that stems from his days as defense secretary under President George Bush. If he becomes vice president, according to a Halliburton official who admires Cheney but asked to remain anonymous, 'the company's government contracts would obviously go through the roof.' "

That was a good bet.

When Cheney reentered the federal service, as the CEO of the second Bush administration, he installed his oldest political comrade, Donald Rumsfeld, as the secretary of defense and his closest ideological ally, Paul Wolfowitz, as the number two man in the Pentagon. After more than a decade of coordinating the privatization of military services from both sides of the public-private partnership, Cheney would in September 2003 claim on NBC's *Meet the Press* that "I have absolutely no influence of, no involvement of, knowledge of in any way, shape, or form, of contracts let by the [U.S. Army] Corps of Engineers or anybody else in the federal government." In a country with a functional media, that statement would have stirred a national outcry. Cheney could not have gone anywhere without being asked, "Do you take us for fools?"—which, of course, he does—and it would be difficult to imagine how he could survive politically. In this era of spin-versus-spin, when Democratic recipients of corporate largesse always pull their punches during discussions about the excesses of Republican recipients of corporate largesse, and where most of the media is more interested in celebrity shenanigans than challenges to the powerful, Cheney continues to be treated as a serious player by most of the media and most of Congress. He is still referred to, with surprising frequency, as a "pub-

A Special Interest in $87 Billion

Vice President Dick Cheney took the lead in public and congressional campaigning in the fall of 2003 to win approval of the Bush administration's request for $87 billion to maintain the occupation of Iraq and other military adventures abroad. Appearing on NBC's *Meet the Press* on September 14, 2003, Cheney said he was "working closely with the Congress in putting the request together," and he described it as a bargain. "It's less money, frankly, than the events of September 11 imposed on us here in the United States," Cheney explained with uncharacteristic enthusiasm.

Cheney had reason to be excited.

While the eventual approval of the $87 billion package represented a political victory for the vice president, it was also a personal coup.

Cheney had a special interest in the request for the $87 billion in additional spending. With an okay from the House and Senate, the proposal allocated roughly $20 billion to reconstruct Iraq, with most of the rest of the money going to cover the costs of the occupation.

That was very good news for Cheney, who, despite his protests to the contrary, retained significant ties to his former employer, the energy and construction conglomerate Halliburton. Halliburton was, of course, the prime beneficiary of military and reconstruction expenditures in Iraq.

At the time of the congressional votes, the U.S. Army

Corps of Engineers had already awarded Halliburton's engineering and construction arm, Brown & Root, a no-bid contract to restore Iraq's oil industry. Halliburton parlayed an initial $37.5 million contract to put out oil field fires into a range of responsibilities that has already run up an estimated $1.7 billion in costs by the fall of 2003. The Army Corps of Engineers would eventually acknowledge that Halliburton could collect as much as $7 billion from taxpayers for its oil field work.

"War is hell, but it has turned into financial heaven for Halliburton," said Senator Frank Lautenberg of New Jersey, who with Congressman Henry Waxman has led the congressional charge to expose details of Halliburton's dealings in Iraq. "This sweetheart, no-bid contract given to Halliburton spikes up by hundreds of millions of dollars each week. It's outrageous."

The outrageousness did not stop there. Another contract between the Pentagon and Halliburton, to manage military bases, had already been revealed to be worth as much as $2 billion. And there were more contracts in the pipeline.

Thus, when Congress approved the $87 billion spending bill, Halliburton was positioned not just to collect maximum payments on its existing contracts, but to go for more gold as the Pentagon opened the dollar spigots. It is important to remember that Halliburton was not set up merely to benefit from the increase in funding for the reconstruction of Iraq's oil industry. Halliburton had also integrated itself into the military side of the operation. As much as one-third of the $3.9 billion-a-month cost of maintaining U.S. troops in Iraq at the time was paid to private contractors such as Halliburton, according to independent analysts.

A *Washington Post* report in August 2003 revealed that "services performed by Halliburton, through its Brown and Root subsidiary, include building and managing military bases, logistical support for the 1,200 intelligence officers hunting Iraqi weapons of mass destruction, delivering mail and producing millions of hot meals. Often dressed in Army fatigues with civilian patches on their shoulders, Halliburton employees and contract personnel have become an integral part of Army life in Iraq."

So it should come as no surprise that when Congress approved another $87 billion to maintain the occupation of Iraq and to pay for reconstruction initiatives, analysts predicted that the value of Halliburton stock would increase. And that's where the congressional vote got particularly interesting for Cheney. As the former CEO of Halliburton, which had seen its stock value plunge as a result of energy-industry turbulence and revelations about its long history of ties to the scandal-plagued Enron Corp., Cheney was in a position to benefit from an uptick in the company's fortunes.

Despite Cheney's claim during that September 2003 *Meet the Press* appearance that he had "severed all my ties with the company, gotten rid of all my financial interest" in Halliburton, Lautenberg argued that Cheney retained significant financial ties to the company. A successful businessman and investor before his election to the Senate, Lautenberg noted that Cheney, who pocketed $44 million for five years of work with Halliburton, continued to collect hundreds of thousands of dollars in deferred salary and retained a significant number of unexercised stock options.

According to an analysis distributed by Lautenberg, if Cheney was to exercise his options, the vice president could

- buy 100,000 shares of Halliburton stock at $54.50 before the end of 2007. That adds up to $5,420,000.
- buy 33,333 shares of Halliburton stock at $28.13 by the end of 2008. That adds up to $937,657.29.
- buy 100,000 shares of Halliburton stock at $39.50 by the end of 2009. That adds up to $3,950,000.

Cheney talks about wanting to donate profits from the sale of these stock options to charity, and he says he will not take tax deductions for such donations. But he could still enjoy the prestige and honor of delivering substantial resources to a favored charity—perhaps the Richard Cheney Vice Presidential Library—and he could also provide Halliburton with a sizable tax deduction.

Unfortunately for Cheney and his former firm, Halliburton shares had been selling for under $25. Thus, for Cheney to be able to cash out, Halliburton stock prices needed to move substantially upward. That prospect was certainly not jeopardized by the decision of Congress to direct millions of dollars in new spending toward projects in which Halliburton was already deeply involved and poised to expand its role.

Did this add up to a conflict of interest? Cheney's office said, "The answer to that is no." But that's because they interpreted the vice president's retention of unexercised stock options as something other than a tie to Halliburton. Lautenberg noted that in addition to sitting on the stock options, the vice president received $205,298 in deferred salary paid by Halliburton in 2001 and $162,392 in deferred salary paid by Halliburton in 2002, and he explained that Cheney was apparently scheduled to collect similar payments in 2003, 2004, and 2005. "The vice president says he does not have any financial ties to Halliburton, but his own financial disclosure filings suggest something else," said Lautenberg. "In 2001 and 2002, Vice President Cheney was paid almost as much in salary from Halliburton as he made as vice president."

Lautenberg was not alone in viewing the deferred salary payments and unexercised stock options as a lingering linkage between Cheney and Halliburton. A Congressional Research Service report described deferred salary and stock options as "among those benefits described by the Office of Government Ethics as 'retained ties' or 'linkages' to one's former employer."

So while the vice president and his aides were busy spinning their way around the question of whether conflicts existed, Lautenberg said, "I ask the vice president to stop dodging the issue with legalese."

The vice president did not take his advice, and Lautenberg and other Senate Democrats attempted to amend the $87 billion spending bill to force Cheney to finally cut what the Congressional Research Service described as "retained ties" and "linkages" to Halliburton. The amendment would have prevented companies with financial ties to Bush, Cheney, and their cabinet secretaries from obtaining Pentagon contracts in Iraq. And it would have required members of the Bush administration who retained stock options to exercise them in ninety days or forfeit the benefits.

Cheney aides claimed all the talk about the vice president's ties to Halliburton was "a political cheap shot." But as the details of Halliburton's sweetheart deals, its overcharging of the U.S. government, and the ever expanding value of its contracts with the Pentagon were revealed, what Cheney aides called a "cheap shot" was starting to look like a smoking gun.

lic servant" and "a man of great integrity" by media and political players who ought to know better. Only a handful of skeptics state the obvious: that the unnamed Halliburton official's prediction has come true. Halliburton contracts have gone through the roof.

And the main reason for that is a war for which Dick Cheney served as head cheerleader. Before the war started, in October 2002, representatives of Vice President Cheney's office reportedly held an "informal" meeting with Halliburton officials to discuss how to get Iraqi oil flowing after a U.S. invasion.

Since the onset of the war in Iraq, Halliburton has become the largest private sector contractor in that country. As of the spring of 2004, it was estimated that Halliburton had collected contracts worth $11 billion for its work in Iraq alone. Some of the most lucrative contracts were obtained without even going through the traditional bidding process, including the March 2003 contract to put out oil well fires that was awarded to Brown & Root by the Army Corps of Engineers. That no-bid contract was made possible by a waiver, granted in January 2003 by the Bush administration, which the *Washington Post* said permitted "government agencies to handpick companies for Iraqi reconstruction projects." After repeated questioning by Congressman Henry Waxman, the Army Corps of Engineers acknowledged that the contract to put out oil well fires—which quickly evolved into a contract to reconstruct Iraq's oil industry—could be worth as much as $7 billion.

Congressman Waxman, a California Democrat who is one of the last old-fashioned watchdogs on Capitol Hill, says of the Iraq contracts, "We know that Halliburton got very special treatment. What we don't know is why." In point of fact, the why is not in question. When he served as secretary of defense, Dick Cheney created a system for dispersing more and more federal money to private contractors with close ties to powerful players in government. When he served as CEO of Halliburton, Cheney created a program to exploit the system. Retired air force colonel Sam Gardiner, a former instructor at the National War College, describes the process as "a patronage system." And, Gardiner told the *New Yorker,* "the system is sick." But what of Dick Cheney? "He doesn't see the difference between public and private interest," says Gardiner. Cheney may not know the difference, but the activist group Citizen Works does. In the spring of 2003, as details of Halliburton's Iraq contracts began to surface, Citizen Works honored Big Business Day by awarding Cheney the "Daddy Warbucks" award for preeminence in corporate war profiteering. The vice president did not attend the ceremony.

Nor did Halliburton scale back its campaign to collect every contract it could. Halliburton's name was becoming shorthand for war profiteering, but the company was not going to veer from the course charted by Cheney. Even after Halliburton was accused of overcharging the Pentagon for meals for troops and gas for military vehicles, and of taking kickbacks from a contractor in Kuwait, the company kept moving higher and higher on the list of the Pentagon's preferred contractors. With predictions that the reconstruction of Iraq could cost as much as $105 billion over the next decade—the *Wall Street Journal* was starting to describe the Iraqi occupation as "the largest government reconstruction effort since Americans helped to rebuild Germany and Japan after World War II"—Halliburton was going for the big score.

And despite the embarrassing headline here and there, its prospects looked good. The Bush-Cheney administration was holding the line against any scaling back of U.S. commitments in Iraq, and Pentagon aides were still peddling the spin that said only Halliburton had the heft and the experience to do the work. The contracts kept coming. Cheney might not be the CEO of the corporation any longer, but as CEO of the U.S.A. he still appeared to be delivering for Halliburton.

2. The other page of Cheney's brief as Halliburton's CEO, the outreach to international clients, was an even more ambitious—and, in many ways, more troubling—enterprise. During

Cheney's tenure at Halliburton, the firm dramatically expanded its overseas operations. When Cheney joined Halliburton, its off-shore projects accounted for 51 percent of revenues; when he left to join the 2000 GOP ticket, the figure had risen to 68 percent. With major contracts in 130 countries, Halliburton had one hundred thousand workers worldwide. And a great deal of the credit for Halliburton's globalization went to one man. Between 1995 and 2000, Cheney was Halliburton's international traveling salesman. And he wasn't making cold calls. As the ranking Republican member of the House Intelligence Committee and secretary of defense, he had gotten to know his way around the world's corridors of power. And unlike other corporate CEOs hustling for contracts and commissions, Cheney had the ability to offer potential clients something more than just pipeline services. Consider what happened when Cheney was asked to join the board of directors of Morgan Stanley, the international banking firm. Traveling in China in 1995 with Morgan Stanley officials, Cheney was able to arrange meetings between the bankers and top government leaders. The journey took place at a tense time, as the Chinese had just staked a claim on an island controlled by the Philippines. The Chinese had erected structures at a location known as Mischief Reef, provoking Philippine president Fidel Ramos to order ships from his country's navy into the disputed waters. Cheney, the old hawk, was suddenly sounding distinctly dovish. Despite the fact that the Chinese had provoked a long-time ally of the United States, the former secretary of defense told a reporter, "I do not really perceive any threat from China to the world or to the region." Thus, Cheney let China off the hook. "Cheney's statement on Mischief Reef was very mischievous," a China expert with ties to Republicans on Capitol Hill subsequently told the *New Republic.* "Saying China is not a threat sent a message to Southeast Asian countries that major parts of the U.S. establishment weren't going along [with their calls to pressure China to withdraw]." Of course, Cheney had no authority to speak for the U.S. government. But his words were still soothing to the ears of the Chinese, so soothing that not long after Cheney left Beijing, China's People's Construction Bank agreed to a major expansion of its joint venture with Morgan Stanley.

Cheney's willingness to use his political prestige to aid Halliburton's business endeavors abroad—and those of other firms that paid him to sit on their boards, such as Morgan Stanley, Lockheed Martin, and Procter & Gamble—became his trademark as a business executive. If there was money to be made, Cheney was more than ready to argue the case for bending policies in favor of the widest corporate latitude. For instance, he became an outspoken critic of unilateral U.S. sanctions against countries that were accused of violating human rights or supporting terrorism. Sanctions did not just hurt dictators abroad, they hurt U.S. businesses, Cheney claimed as he pushed for the review of U.S. restrictions on trade with Libya, Iran, and Iraq. Cheney's opposition to sanctions may have made good sense from a humanitarian standpoint, but it made even better sense from a Halliburton standpoint. Most of the countries against which the United States and other Western countries maintained sanctions had underdeveloped or damaged infrastructures for extracting, processing, and exporting natural resources. One of the first steps taken by leaders of cash-strapped countries when sanctions were eased was to contract with companies that could help them get oil, or natural gas, or coal out of the ground and onto the open market. It just happened that this was what Halliburton was good at. It also happened that Halliburton did not have many qualms about working with local reprobates.

Indeed, when Halliburton employees rolled into Iraq in March 2003, side by side with the uniformed branch of the military-industrial complex, they should have had an easy time finding their way around the country. After all, they weren't entirely new to the territory. According to United Nations records, Halliburton's Dresser-Rand and Ingersoll Dresser Pump Co. subsidiaries sold pipeline equipment, spare parts for oil facilities, and water and sewage treatment pumps to Saddam Hussein's government. Halliburton's subsidiaries even inked a contract to repair an Iraqi oil terminal that had been destroyed during the Gulf War—presumably by U.S. forces. Some of Halliburton's activities in Iraq were legal, under the "oil-for-food" programs implemented by the United Nations Security Council to ease the human suffering that had resulted from the oil embargo and related sanctions imposed after the invasion of Kuwait. Some were more questionable; for instance, Halliburton's deal to repair the oil terminal was ultimately blocked by the United States government because it was determined to violate the sanctions regime.

When Cheney nominated himself for vice president in 2000, Halliburton's Iraqi connections became a political liability. It was difficult to suggest that the Clinton administration had been lax about preventing "rogue nations" such as Iraq from attaining materials to develop weapons of mass destruction when you were the boss of a company that had supplied equipment to Iraq and enriched the regime. As the *Washington Post* noted long after the campaign was done, "U.S. and European officials acknowledged that the expanded production [of oil] also increased

Saddam Hussein's capacity to siphon off money for weapons, luxury goods and palaces. Security Council diplomats estimate that Iraq may be skimming off as much as 10 percent of the proceeds from the oil-for-food program." Considering the fact that Iraq exported oil worth more than $40 billion during the first four years of the oil-for-food initiative, the boys in Baghdad enjoyed a considerable infusion of cash thanks to the loosening of restrictions and the help of Halliburton and other contractors. Halliburton made out okay as well. During the time that Cheney was chairman and chief executive officer of the company, the firm's subsidiaries signed contracts with the Iraqis that were worth almost $30 million.

What looked like good money when Cheney was CEO, however, did not look good when he was a candidate. When Cheney was asked in 2000 about his company's "rogue nation" partnerships, he admitted that Halliburton did business with Iran, Libya—where Halliburton's dealings had in 1995 cost the company $3.8 million in fines for violating U.S. trade sanctions—and just about every other country that could clear a check. But Cheney, who was closely associated with neoconservative groups that had criticized the Clinton-Gore administration for failing to get tough with Iraq, denied that he had any connection to Saddam. "Iraq's different," he said. Appearing on ABC-TV's *This Week* program in July 2000, the vice presidential candidate was questioned by Sam Donaldson: "I'm told, and correct me if I'm wrong, that Halliburton, through subsidiaries, was actually trying to do business in Iraq."

"No, no," Cheney replied in the cool, almost off-the-cuff manner that he always adopts when the truth might need a little stretching. "I had a firm policy that we wouldn't do anything in Iraq, even arrangements that were supposedly legal. We've not done any business in Iraq since UN sanctions were imposed on Iraq in 1990, and I had a standing policy that I wouldn't do that."

Unfortunately for Cheney, the UN kept records. When he appeared on *This Week* the following month, Cheney was scrambling. He said he hadn't been aware that "we inherited two joint ventures with Ingersoll-Rand that were selling some parts into Iraq, but we divested ourselves of those interests."

Just to be clear here, the parts weren't being sold "into Iraq," they were being sold *to* Iraq. And the divestiture was not exactly immediate. Both the Ingersoll Dresser Pump Co. and Ingersoll-Rand subsidiaries dramatically increased their dealings in Iraq during Cheney's tenure as Halliburton's CEO. There has never been any evidence to suggest that they were divested because of their ties to Iraq.

And what of the claim by Cheney that he did not know about the Halliburton-Iraq connection? James Perrella, former chairman of Ingersoll-Rand, told the *Washington Post* that based on his knowledge of how Halliburton and its subsidiaries worked, Cheney had to have known. "Oh, definitely," Perrella said of Cheney, "he was aware of the business."

For Cheney, who sells himself as the detail man who just can't stop asking questions, it will always be difficult to claim that he didn't know what Halliburton was up to in its global enterprises. And that means that he will, for the rest of his life, face lingering questions about dirty deeds done in Halliburton's name.

That's because few corporations in the history of the world have ever arranged and maintained more deals with dictators than Halliburton did when Cheney was in charge. Cheney explained these partnerships by saying, "The good Lord didn't see fit to put oil and gas where there are democratic regimes friendly to the United States." And that line of reasoning seemed, at least in his mind, to justify any deal that could be made. The company was proudly partnered, for instance, with the military regime of Myanmar (Burma) on a pair of energy pipeline projects that, according to EarthRights, an international human rights group, exploited indentured labor and sanctioned the use of violence against indigenous peoples who objected to the forced relocation of entire villages.

Indeed, when Halliburton comes to a country, it's a good bet that trouble will follow. One of the ugliest stories of Halliburton's globe-trotting comes out of Nigeria, the oil-and-gas-rich West African country where the brutal dictatorship of Sani Abacha garnered a good deal of attention for jailing and executing environmentalists—including playwright Ken Saro-Wiwa—who were displeased by its willingness to allow the government's international oil industry partners to dislocate communities and despoil vast stretches of the countryside. Abacha looked like someone with whom Halliburton could do business. The price that Halliburton and its partners in an international corsortium had to pay was high—they are alleged to have paid a $180 million bribe to the Abacha government—but it was a pittance compared with the potential payout. The liquefied natural gas plant they planned to build was valued at as much as $6 billion. Things went swimmingly until the Abacha dictatorship began to crumble and details of its dealings with companies such as Halliburton leaked out. One of Halliburton's partners was a French firm, and in 2003, one of the most respected jurists in France launched an investigation of charges of corporate corruption. The judge, Renaud van Ruymbeke, caused a stir in early 2004 when he said he might call Cheney to France to answer questions regarding any involvement the vice president might have had in the alleged bribing of the Nigerians. Around the same time, the U.S. Department of Justice and the Securities & Exchange Commission opened investigations of the Nigerian scandal, as did the new Nigerian government. Halliburton said recently that whatever happened in Nigeria was commenced by an independent company that was later bought by Halliburton. Typically, media coverage has been tepid, although the *Boston Globe* editorialized in February 2004, "If such payments were made and Cheney approved them, he could be guilty of violating the U.S. Foreign Corrupt Practices Act. If the payments were made and he did not know about them, he could not have been a hands-on leader of the conglomerate. The nation, in any case, deserves answers before it votes in November if, as President Bush has indicated, he retains Cheney as his running mate."

3. Global capitalism can be a risky business, especially for a company that works in the remote "Wild West" corners of the world where multibillion-dollar oil and natural gas stakes are discovered and developed.

But Dick Cheney's connections with people in powerful places made it possible for him to take a lot of the risk out of Halliburton's international engagements. Like another company with ties to people in high places and a penchant for distributing hefty campaign contributions at election time—Enron—Halliburton found some deep-pocket lenders that were willing to provide loan guarantees and insurance for foreign projects that didn't necessarily look good "on paper." The U.S. Overseas Private Investment Corporation (OPIC) and the Export-Import Bank, both of which are funded by U.S. taxpayers, provided roughly $100 million in direct loans and loan guarantees for international projects in which Halliburton was involved during the five years before Dick Cheney became the company's CEO. During the five years when Cheney was in charge, the figure leapt to $1.5 billion.

While some firms wait years for the financing to support overseas projects in which they are partnered, once Cheney arrived, the money seemed always to be flowing for international endeavors that would enrich Halliburton. There was $88 million for an Angolan project in 1996, $150 million for projects in Algeria in 1997, $531 million for a project in Mexico in 1998, $66 million for another project in Angola in 1999, $400 million more for the project in Mexico in 2000, $36 million to back up an earlier loan of $266 million for a project in Russia in 2000, and $100 million in insurance for a project in Bangladesh in 2000—all backed up not by private sector banks, but by the taxpayers of the United States.

The U.S. Overseas Private Investment Corporation and the Export-Import Bank were set up to help American firms expand their business abroad, in hopes that such expansions would create jobs at home while building goodwill around the world. Those intended benefits served as the justification for using tax dollars to guarantee investments in potentially risky overseas endeavors. But the projects in which Halliburton involved itself often seemed to lack the noble purpose that the OPIC and Export-Import Bank brochures describe. For instance, that Russian project involved a scheme to refurbish a Siberian oil field that was owned by the Tyumen Oil Co., which in turn is controlled by a

Russian conglomerate known as the Alfa Group. The Center for Public Integrity, which obtained documents regarding the deal and Tyumen, published a report describing Halliburton's Russian partner as a "company whose roots are imbedded in a legacy of KGB and Communist Party corruption, as well as drug trafficking and organized crime funds." The Russian company has hotly disputed those claims.

But meanwhile, others were saying that the recipients of the Export–Import Bank loans to support the oil field project—and to guarantee an infusion of $292 million into Halliburton's accounts—were shady. Who was saying that, exactly? Well, BP-Amoco, for one. According to the CIA report, the giant oil and gas production company charged that Tyumen committed fraudulent acts and corrupted a bankruptcy proceeding to steal an oil field from the legitimate owners, which included BP-Amoco. BP-Amoco was so exercised about Tyumen's actions that it passed details of the company's alleged links with Russian–organized crime interests to the U.S. Central Intelligence Agency. The CIA classified the materials as "secret." But when the CIA briefed the Export-Import Bank about Tyumen, it reportedly told the bankers that the information contained in the BP-Amoco materials "tracked" with information the agency had obtained separately regarding the Russian firm.

It would seem that a project involving Tyumen might not have looked like the safest investment. And, indeed, that was how most bankers saw it. That was also how the U.S. State Department saw it. The State Department took a dim view of the Siberian project, arguing that the deal ran against the "national interest." The CIA agreed. That should have doomed the deal. But Halliburton played the Cheney card. After he came to the company, Cheney dramatically ramped up the firm's D.C. lobbying operation—doubling Halliburton's influence-peddling budget to $600,000 by 1999—and according to the records of Dave Gribben, who headed Halliburton's Washington office, the focus was on nontraditional pressure points, such as OPIC and the Export-Import Bank. Gribben was not Halliburton's lobbyist in chief, however; that was Cheney's job. Cheney reportedly made personal trips to Washington to lobby on behalf of the Tyumen project, cozying up to Export-Import Bank chairman James Harmon, who in April 2000 overrode the recommendations of the State Department and the CIA and agreed to front Tyumen $489 million. That was the largest amount of money ever loaned by the bank to a Russian company, but most of it would be coming home—in the form of $292 million in U.S.-taxpayer-guaranteed payments to Halliburton.

The Tyumen loan guarantee would be the last big catch reeled in by Cheney for the company he had joined after that fateful fly-fishing trip to New Brunswick five years earlier. The time had come to go back through the revolving door. He had served in three White Houses, in progressively more powerful positions. Now, he wanted to be in charge. Cheney knew the voters would never give him the title he craved, but he knew how to get the power that went with it. He had arrived in Texas at a convenient moment, just after George W. Bush assumed the governorship in 1995, and he had insinuated himself into the inner circles of the boy and his father. Cheney was certain that the family could deliver the Republican nomination to George W., and he thought there was a reasonable chance that Bush could win in November. There would not be many more opportunities like this one. Cheney had to be on board. As in the past, he let it be known that he was willing to perform the scut work of the campaign. He gladly accepted the time-consuming, high-pressure, and historically ego-crushing job of selecting Bush's running mate. Halliburton's board graciously allowed its chief executive to cut back on his duties briefly in order to perform a little service to the Republican Party—which in their eyes was synonymous with the country. After all, helping out the next president could only make Cheney more valuable to the company. But Cheney knew he was not coming back. In May, he quietly sold Halliburton stock holdings worth $5 million. The sale should have been a signal, but no one recognized that he was cashing out. It would be two more months before Dick Cheney would nominate himself for vice president.

CEO, prime minister, or commissar?: Cheney picked himself as George W. Bush's vice president, chief of energy policy, and political czar. Then he staffed the White House with his cronies. According to Paul O'Neill, the old friend Cheney recruited to be Treasury Secretary, Cheney's White House has embraced "brazen ideology" that is "not penetrable by facts." But as Cheney has said, "Confrontation fits our strategy. Polarization often has very beneficial results." (2001)

CHAPTER 7

UNNATURAL SELECTION

I reached out to a distinguished and experienced statesman to lead the search.

> —George W. Bush, 2000, explaining his choice of
> Dick Cheney to help him select a running mate

The more I see evidence he is wiggling to become a candidate, the more I smell a rat.

> —A Republican aide, 2000, discussing
> Cheney's process of self-selection

The suggestion that somehow, because this was a close election, we should fundamentally change our beliefs I just think is silly.

> —Vice President–elect Dick Cheney, 2001

Everyone knew that George W. Bush would need a minder. It was not that he was stupid per se, just careless. He had broken just about everything he had ever touched—including four oil industry firms and the state of Texas. In a rare moment of sober reflection, George W. had explained to a reporter, "I'm basically a media creation. I've never done anything. I've worked for my dad. I worked in the oil business. But that's not the kind of profile you have to have to get elected to public office." The brother with the proper profile was John Ellis Bush (Jeb), whom pundits had been touting since the 1980s as "the next generation Bush." Jeb was the brother who was supposed to reoccupy the White House in 2000. Unfortunately, the voters of Florida were not informed of Jeb's timetable. When Floridians chose not to elect Jeb as their governor in 1994, they created a huge problem for the Bush clan. Jeb would not be able to update his résumé until 1998, which did not leave nearly enough time to prepare for the coming presidential race. So the family was forced to turn to George W., who with the help of his political Svengali, Karl Rove, and the "Republican revolution" tide had been swept into the Texas governor's mansion in 1994. If the Bushes were to have a horse in the 2000 race, it was going to be George W.

The problem was that George W. had never bothered to prepare for the presidency. Despite Rove's comic attempts to make it appear as if Bush were bilingual, the governor struggled, often painfully, with the English language. ("Born with a silver foot in his mouth," is how former Texas governor Ann Richards described George W.'s way with words.) He had no international experience. He had no Washington experience. He had no military experience—unless, of course, credit is given for time spent AWOL from the Texas Air National Guard sinecure that had been created to keep him safe from the fight in Vietnam. His business experience was a tragic record of one failure after another, from which he had to be rescued at each bad turn by increasingly substantial infusions of cash from increasingly dubious domestic and foreign "friends" of his politically powerful father. He had attained the governorship by fronting a campaign that raised heaping piles of special-interest money and spent it to trash the reputation of an abler and more honorable foe. He then proceeded to create a fiscal crisis so overwhelming that when asked about his state's looming deficit during the 2000 campaign, Bush admitted, "I hope I'm not around to deal with it."

Even among Bush's top aides, there was a consciousness that this man was not ready for political prime time. Reporters covering the early stages of the 2000 campaign quickly became familiar with the Bush team's meticulous monitoring of the candidate's pronouncements; when he said something inane, incorrect, or simply incomprehensible, Ari Fleischer, Karl Rove, or another member of the communications cleanup crew would appear instantly to "clarify" what Bush meant. If a reporter dared detail the candidate's all-too-obvious weaknesses, there would be a 6:00 A.M. call from Karen "Hell Hath No Fury Like" Hughes. And the Bush team had no qualms about working its way up the media food chain to the executive suites, where the CEOs of communications conglomerates did not need to be reminded that if Bush actually did become president, he would be appointing members of the Federal Communications Commission.

The Bush for President campaign was the ultimate spin job. Yet even as Bush bumbled early in the battle, losing a couple of primaries to seat-of-the-pants challenger John McCain, the better-funded and better-disciplined Bush crew grew increasingly confident that they could indeed spin their man-child candidate into a Republican nominee. What worried responsible Republicans and conservative commentators, however, was the prospect that the party was about to gamble its future on a man who, in the words of *National Review* writer Richard Brookhiser, came off as "a fairly unpleasant fifty-three-year-old teen-ager." Even George Will, the syndicated columnist who never met a Republican presidential nominee he didn't apologize for, worried in print that Bush manifested "an atmosphere of adolescence . . . a carelessness, even a recklessness, perhaps born of things having gone a bit too easily so far."

No one was more aware of these concerns than George Herbert Walker Bush. The former president wanted nothing more than to put the Bush brand back on the White House, but he recognized that his son lacked a certain gravitas. What father Bush knew, however, was that gravitas could be attached to a lightweight candidate, in the form of a heavyweight running mate. Having served as vice president himself, and having blown a vice presidential selection process when he tapped the differently abled Dan Quayle in 1988, the elder Bush believed that finding the right running mate was the essential task that lay before his son's campaign in the spring and early summer of 2000. It was not just a matter of political positioning; the former president, a man of government whose own record of experience stood in marked contrast with that of his slow-starter son, recognized that the pressures of the presidency were such that the younger Bush would need a second in command with the skills to steer the new administration around the potholes that had wrecked the first terms of better-prepared men. As veteran journalist James Klurfeld observed, there was a consciousness on the part of "Papa Bush and the handlers" that it was going to be necessary to put someone "in charge of the kid's government." The former president impressed upon his son the importance of selecting the right person to manage the search for a running mate; it must be someone at once savvy about the ways of Washington, well connected within the Republican Party and its broad corporate contributor base, and completely loyal to the Bush clan. That pretty much narrowed the field to Dick Cheney and Donald Rumsfeld.

But Rumsfeld was a showboater. Cheney, who had already made himself useful to the campaign by managing foreign policy and defense briefings for the candidate, was always offering to help. Why not Dick? So it was that, after his campaign had dispensed with the annoying McCain challenge, George W. Bush sat down with Dick Cheney to discuss the vice presidential selection process.

At the outset, Bush had specifically asked Cheney whether the former defense secretary wanted to be considered as a candidate. Had Cheney answered yes, someone else would have been given the responsibility of running the selection process. But, of course, Cheney had known since his intern days on Capitol Hill that if you want a job, you don't hand off the responsibility for evaluating the candidates to someone else. So, as Bush recalled it, Cheney responded with an emphatic no. A few days later, Bush quietly announced that Cheney would head his "thorough and dignified" review of potential running mates. "I reached out to a distinguished and experienced statesman to lead the search," Bush explained. "For months, we worked closely together to review the qualifications of many impressive candidates. As we worked to evaluate the strengths of others, I saw firsthand Dick Cheney's outstanding judgment. As we considered many different credentials, I benefited from his keen insight."

Cheney was at it again, taking on the thankless job and then making himself the essential confidant of the person who would make the final decision. As Bush reviewed the pluses and minuses of potential running mates—McCain, former Missouri senator John Danforth, Tennessee senator Fred Thompson, Pennsylvania governor Tom Ridge—Cheney was at the table, quietly offering his subtly self-serving insights. It was Cheney who put the candidates through the hoops, demanding that they pull together masses of documents, including health records and details of past indiscretions, for his review. And when Bush met with the likely suspects, there were no man-to-man, one-on-one discussions. Cheney was in the room as well, asking-probing and potentially disqualifying questions. Amazingly, considering his track record, most of the participants in the process actually believed that it was a serious endeavor. But a few of the contenders began to develop suspicions. As the time for a decision approached in late July, one of the officials who was reportedly on Bush's short list confided to a wire service reporter, "It took 50, 60, 70 hours to pull all that paper together and all that. . . . I just hope it wasn't a waste of time." When Cheney's name came into contention, another candidate said, "I have to believe them when they say he emerged late, but it still makes you shake your head."

It had been a waste of time. And it was right to shake heads. Cheney was narrowing the process toward an inevitable decision. He focused attention at the end on Danforth, an affable former senator who remained popular in the important swing state of Missouri. Barely a week before Bush was expected to announce his choice, Danforth was summoned to Chicago for a closed-door meeting with Bush and Cheney. Speculation about the former senator spiked in the media. But Danforth had never been a "made" member of the Bush organization, and damned if he hadn't written a vitriolic little book titled *Resurrection: The Confirmation of Clarence Thomas,* in which he had trashed law professor Anita Hill, women's groups, and everyone else who had questioned the 1991 nomination of the conservative ideologue to the Supreme Court. With Bush running as a "compassionate conservative" who hoped to downplay the culture clash issues that had created a serious gender gap for the GOP, Danforth was suddenly portrayed as a risky choice—with CNN reporting that an unnamed official close to the selection process had referred to the quiet and accommodating Danforth as too "polarizing" and "not a good match in terms of the moderate suburban mom vote." So there they were, Bush and Cheney, with the Republican National Convention coming up and no one left to nominate for vice president. Or so it seemed. Actually, weeks before, Cheney had gotten on the phone to papa Bush, and according to the back chatter within the campaign, the two old comrades—whose relationship stretched back to the days when Rumsfeld and Cheney had gotten Gerald Ford to appoint Bush as director of the Central Intelligence Agency—tossed around the idea of a Bush-Cheney ticket. News reports revealed that "a GOP source close to both Dick Cheney and Texas Gov. George W. Bush" had said that former president Bush was "extremely high on Cheney." (After the choice was finally made, the joke among Republican insiders was that Cheney was a "prudent" pick, a reference to the father's much parodied "wouldn't be prudent" catchphrase.)

With the former president giving his trademark thumbs-up, this deal was about to be closed. Two days after the Chicago meeting with Danforth, Cheney underwent a complete physical and got as clean a bill of health as can be expected for a fifty-nine-year-old man who had suffered three heart attacks and undergone quadruple bypass surgery. Then he switched his voter registration from Texas to Wyoming—dispensing with the complication created by the Constitution's requirement that the president and vice president be residents of different states. Now the smiles were beginning to appear on the faces of the Republican insiders who knew Cheney. He had pulled it off. As CNN reported on July 24, the day before Bush and Cheney were scheduled to make the long-awaited announcement of the 2000 ticket, "one longtime party official who knows Cheney well said he was surprised that details of Cheney's recent movements have been so easy to track, including his decision to change his voter registration and his decision to undergo an extensive medical examination last week. 'Dick knows how to keep a secret,' this official said. 'The more I see evidence he is wiggling to become a candidate, the more I smell a rat.' "

Bingo!

On July 25, 2000, in Austin, Texas, George W. Bush announced that during one of his early July meetings with Cheney, it had dawned on him that "the best candidate might be sitting next to me." How about that? What a coincidence that the person sitting next to him was Dick Cheney.

"I didn't pick Dick Cheney because of Wyoming's three electoral votes—although we want and will work hard to earn them," Bush joked to the assembled reporters. Then he got serious. "I picked him because he is without a doubt fully capable of being president of the United States. . . ."

On that point, Cheney was in complete agreement. And so were a lot of other observers of the burgeoning relationship between the "unpleasant 53-year-old teen-ager" and the man who had been brought in to run things. Appearing on CBS's *Face the Nation,* veteran Republican operative Scott Reed did not even attempt to portray Cheney as a deferent second in command. "He'd probably almost be like a prime minister," Reed said of the role Cheney would fill in a Bush administration. It was a prescient prediction, especially if the model is that of Great Britain or most other Western democracies, where the prime minister runs the government and a figurehead monarch or president attends to ceremonial duties.

"I am glad to be back in the arena," Cheney told the Republican National Convention on August 2, after the delegates had confirmed what most reporters insisted on describing as Bush's "surprise" choice. The arena to which Cheney referred was not the political competition that he and Bush would join as an oddly matched tag team over the next four and a half months (three for the official campaign, one and a half to warp Florida's results in their favor). For Cheney, the campaign would be a minor annoyance, in which he would spend most of his time talking to small audiences of loyal Republicans in remote, barely disclosed locations. During the campaign, he would draw only two spasms of press attention. One came when Bush referred to *New York Times* reporter Adam Clymer as a "major league asshole" and Cheney chirped, "Big-time!" The other saw Cheney deliver the most ironic line of an election season that was not short on irony: during a discussion on the state of the economy that was part of the sole vice presidential debate, Democrat Joe Lieberman got a giggle with a reference to Cheney's Halliburton largesse by saying, "I'm pleased to see, Dick, that you're better off than you were eight years ago." Cheney looked at him with a straight face and said, "I can tell you that the government had absolutely nothing to do with it."

But anyone who knew Dick Cheney recognized that poking fun at reporters and lying in debates was not what he was talking about when he spoke of how glad he was to be "back in the arena."

The arena was the White House.

Cheney could not wait to take charge. While Bush was con-

The (Extreme) Right Choice

When Dick Cheney selected himself to be George W. Bush's running mate in July 2000, media reports often identified him as a congenial, moderate figure. He was even described as "a friendly, gentlemanly candidate who is not an ideologue." Not an ideologue? Don't tell that to the arbiters of reaction. The religious Right was in heaven. The cultural conservatives were singing his praises. The right guard celebrated their party's deliverance from the disturbing threat that conservatives might be required to show some compassion. No one who had ever caucused with the conservatives believed that Dick Cheney was a moderate. They recognized him as the right choice . . . the extreme right choice:

Dick Cheney is even more conservative than me.
—Former House Speaker Newt Gingrich

[Cheney is] Tom DeLay with table manners.
—Syndicated columnist Robert Novak, comparing Cheney with the Texan who serves as the point man for the Republican Right in Congress

The Republican ticket is now exquisitely balanced: a man of the center [Bush] who doesn't alienate the right has chosen a man of the right [Cheney] who doesn't alienate the center.
—William F. Buckley's *National Review* magazine

Bush made what conservatives have to regard as the best veep choice a Republican nominee has made since Eisenhower tapped Nixon.

—*National Review* columnists John Miller and
Ramesh Ponnuru, delivering what is
apparently a compliment

George W. Bush's announcement that he has asked Dick Cheney to be his running mate is, in my mind, an excellent move—one that will additionally energize many camps within the Republican Party.

—Reverend Jerry Falwell

[Cheney is] a moral man.

—Christian Coalition founder Pat Robertson, who,
when there was talk in 2004 of dropping Cheney
from the GOP ticket, intervened to declare,
"To dump him, I think, would be a tragic mistake"

The naming of Dick Cheney as Governor George W. Bush's running mate sends an unmistakable message: There will be no departure from the Republican Party's principled stand in defense of the sanctity of life.

—Family Research Council

Conservatives are thrilled that Bush, a centrist establishment Republican, has selected a solid conservative to balance the ticket. . . . Dick Cheney looks like them [the centrist establishment] but he sounds like one of us—a principled conservative.

> —Richard Viguerie, fund-raising strategist
> for the Republican Right

Governor Bush has not only chosen well, he has chosen the best of men. . . . Dick's estimable voting record in the House of Representatives was a solidly and consistently conservative one: categorically and unambiguously pro-life, pro-military and strong defense, and pro-tax cuts. In fact, Dick's voting record is the kind of pattern that historians and political scientists will clearly label as having belonged to a solid Reagan conservative.

> —Gary Bauer, former head of the Family
> Research Council, who had challenged
> Bush in the Republican primaries on
> the grounds that the Texan was too liberal

Only on Bauer's final point might Cheney disagree. When he served in the House, Cheney sometimes complained that the Reagan administration leaned a little too far to the left. During negotiations over the 1986 tax bill, the Reagan White House found some room for compromise with powerful House Way and Means Committee chairman Dan Rostenkowski. Then congressman Cheney is reported to have angrily accused the president of "selling out to Rostenkowski."

tent to wait patiently for the Supreme Court to confirm his selection as president, Cheney jetted into Washington to stake his claim. Running Bush's transition team out of rented office space, Cheney established himself, in the words of *Washington Post* writer Dana Milbank, "as Bush's spokesman, his legislative liaison, his personnel manager, and his strategist—in short, his chief executive." Cheney was grabbing so much power so quickly that he worked himself up to another heart attack—his first since 1988. But he was not going to let a life-and-death incident slow him down. After doctors placed a stent in a clogged artery, he was out of the hospital within days and, skipping the bed rest, back at the job of shaping his, er, Bush's administration.

The new vice president brought the old team back together. Rumsfeld, Wolfowitz, Scooter Libby, all the old hands from Cheney's Department of Defense got new jobs. A pal from the Ford administration, Alcoa CEO Paul O'Neill, would take charge of the Department of the Treasury. Cheney was re-creating the circles in which he had been comfortable in the past. Jim Stevenson, an aviation writer who had covered Cheney as secretary of defense, saw a familiar pattern developing. This was the Cheney he knew, the guy who had a tendency to "surround himself with a few close associates and they'd huddle together like musk ox protecting their young." But this time, Cheney was building an entire administration. There had to be places for old rivals like Colin Powell, who could bring a measure of political credibility to an administration that the majority of Americans had not supported in November. Cheney had had his differences with Powell during the first Bush administration, when the then chairman of the Joint Chiefs of Staff had turned the president against some of Cheney's loonier schemes regarding Iraq. Powell had even had the audacity to ask, in a meeting with the president and members of the cabinet, whether the liberation of Kuwait was a goal worthy of the certain sacrifice of American lives. For that, Cheney had taken him aside and explained sternly, "Colin, you're chairman of the Joint Chiefs. You're not secretary of state. You're not national security adviser. And you're not secretary of defense. So stick to military matters." The scolding had a distinct "I'm in charge" sound to it, but in the first Bush administration, that claim of authority had been open to debate.

In the second Bush administration, there was no debate. Powell would be the secretary of state, but as he would learn when he raised questions about the faulty evidence on which the case for war with Iraq was being made, that title referred to a very different job from the one James Baker held in the first Bush administration. This time, in matters of diplomacy, foreign relations, and, above all, war making, Cheney's supremacy would be far more clearly defined. The vice president's brief would not be limited to the global stage. "To get an idea of how Cheney will influence the new administration, it's instructive to draw a corporate-style organization chart of the transition," wrote Milbank. "The dozens of workers are divided into groups: legal, policy, strategy, administration, communications, press. Each group's head reports to [Cheney confidant] Clay Johnson, who in turn reports to Cheney, who answers only to Bush. The only person who reports directly to Bush other than Cheney, transition officials say, is White House staff chief." Card, Milbank noted, "also answers to Cheney." Cheney aides were peddling the line that the model for the new administration would be "a corporate one: Bush as the nation's chairman of the board, Cheney as America's chief executive."

That was a decent comparison, but the prime ministerial analogy that Scott Reed had advanced around the time Cheney was nominated would turn out to be a more appropriate one. Bush was never the complete cipher that his most virulent critics believed or that his most concerned supporters feared. He had a decent education. He had grown up with a man who knew his way around the federal govenment as well as anyone in America, and he still spoke by phone with his father, sometimes two or three times a day. When big decisions were made about whom to place in cabinet posts, and later about policy, the president was always consulted. But the consultations invariably had a perfunctory character, as when the British prime minister informs the queen of the actions he or she is about to take. Thinking that Cheney would be concerned about Bush's disengagement from his own presidency, Paul O'Neill suggested again and again that the president needed to be exposed to more perspectives, brought into more debates, offered more options, and reminded that he had choices. Only over time would O'Neill come to recognize that he was expressing his ideas to the wrong man. "I realized why Dick just nodded along when I said all this, over and over, and nothing ever changed," explained O'Neill, who had finally come to understand that the White House operated the way it did "because this is the way Dick likes it." In his prime ministerial role, it was Cheney, not Bush, who set the administration's combative tone from the start. Rejecting suggestions that an administration that had lost the popular vote in 2000 and that would have to work with two closely divided houses of Congress should govern in a conciliatory, centrist manner, Cheney appeared on CBS's *Face the Nation* program on the day before he and Bush were sworn in and declared, "The suggestion that somehow, because this was a close election, we should fundamentally change our beliefs I just think is silly."

Bush, the ceremonial leader, could give the feel-good inaugural speech about restoring to Washington honest discourse. Cheney, the prime minister, was throwing down the gauntlet. The Republicans had been elected—or, rather, almost elected—on a platform and, Cheney said, "we have no intention at all of backing off it." It was Cheney, above all others, who would see that there was no backsliding. As the prime minister, he would personally manage the most important portfolios.

In an oil-powered administration, there would be no more critical domestic responsibility than the setting of energy policy. So Cheney would head the National Energy Policy Development Group, the so-called energy task force, to which he would appoint all sixty-three members—twenty-seven of them from the oil and gas industry, seventeen from the nuclear industry, sixteen from the electrical utilities, and seven from coal-mining and -processing concerns. The commission, operating under an unprecedented cloak of secrecy, would by May 2001 produce what the *Washington Monthly* referred to as an "all-drilling no-conservation" national energy plan that called for developing 1,300 new coal-fired power plants; providing $33 billion in subsidies and tax cuts to encourage increased nuclear, oil, and coal production; massive deregulation of existing industries; and, famously, the opening of the Arctic National Wildlife Refuge to oil drilling. Cheney's congressional scourge, U.S. representative Henry Waxman, began pressing immediately for the release of documents related to the task force's deliberations—Waxman had a hunch that the proposals submitted by energy industry lobbyists to the vice president would track just about precisely with the official recommendations and the unofficial interventions of Cheney and others associated with the endeavor. The White House refused to release even the names of the lobbyists and corporate CEOs with whom Cheney had met. That brought the nonpartisan investigatory arm of Congress, the Government Accounting Office, into the fight. While some documents were eventually handed over, the administration continued to refuse to release the majority of them. The GAO's lawsuit, which would have forced full disclosure, was dismissed by a Bush-Cheney administration appointee to the federal bench, U.S. district judge John Bates.

Notably, Cheney is also a key player in the administration's program to reshape the federal judiciary. The vice president travels regularly to Capitol Hill to assure conservative Republicans in the Senate that the White House will keep sending extreme right-wing nominees to the Hill and keep attacking Democrats for failing to confirm them. Senate Judiciary Committee member Jeff Sessions, the Alabama Republican who is often the administration's point man in nomination fights, said after one Cheney-led pep rally in 2002, "The White House, I'm convinced, is confident and bullish and determined to push this issue, as we are in the Senate." There's a reason for the bullishness of the Cheney-led White House on this issue. While there can be particular side benefits to packing the courts with friendly conservatives—as the energy task force secrecy ruling well illustrates—the primary purpose of Cheney's watch on the judiciary is political. Elected as a "compassionate conservative" administration, the Bush-Cheney White House still attempts to appear moderate on some issues, which causes concern among social conservatives who have always been wary of the Bush family's roots in the New England moderate Republican tradition. Che-

Kenny's Boy

In the spring of 2001, the severity of the California energy emergency had inspired demands for government action, and Enron had a problem. Officials in California were arguing that federal price caps on wholesale energy sales would prevent profiteering and stabilize wildly fluctuating energy markets, and even some Republicans were saying that caps made sense. But the caps would cost Enron—which had come to dominate energy markets by taking advantage of deregulation—a fortune.

Enron CEO Kenneth Lay knew he needed high-level help. So he arranged to meet with a man who had headed a corporation with extensive business ties to Enron and had been a prime recipient of Enron's political largesse. Vice President Dick Cheney cleared his calendar for an April 17 private meeting with Lay regarding what aides described as "energy policy matters" and "the energy crisis in California." At the meeting, Lay handed Cheney a memo that read in part: "The administration should reject any attempt to reregulate wholesale power markets by adopting price caps. . . ."

The day after he met with Lay, Cheney gave a rare phone interview to the *Los Angeles Times* that had one recurrent theme: Price caps were out of the question. Dismissing the strategy as "short-term political relief for the politicians," Cheney declared bluntly, "I don't see that as a possibility."

Cheney's prognosis was flawed; within days, the Federal Energy Regulatory Commission agreed to price caps, and the markets calmed down. But Cheney was undeterred in his drive to deliver for Enron. The Houston-based firm enjoyed a level of vice presidential attention during the Bush-Cheney team's first year that included explicit support of Enron's choices for key regulatory positions, intervention in the affairs of a foreign government, and the structuring of an energy policy task force to allow Enron and other corporations to effectively set policy. Indeed, so close was the Cheney-Enron relationship that members of Congress began to ask whether ethical and legal lines were crossed. Cheney erected a stone wall, refusing to discuss his meetings with Lay or others and fighting in the courts to prevent the release of documents related to those meetings. "Cheney says he is refusing to provide information to the Congress as a matter of principle. He told the *Today* show that he wants to 'protect the ability of the President and the Vice President to get unvarnished information and advice from any source we want,' " noted former White House counsel John Dean. "That sounds all too familiar to me. I worked for Richard Nixon."

Less than ten days after he became vice president—promising that a Bush-Cheney administration would "restore decency and integrity to the Oval Office"—Cheney took charge of the administration's energy policy task force, the National Energy Policy Development Group. No initiative interested Enron more, and Cheney welcomed the company's active participation in its deliberations. Cheney was hardly a stranger to the company. He had chaired Halliburton, a Texas-based oil services and construction conglomerate whose subsidiary Brown & Root helped build Houston's Enron Field, and his return to politics—after he selected himself to be Bush's running mate—benefited from Enron-linked contributions that helped pay for the Bush-Cheney campaign, the Florida recount fight fund, and the inauguration. Cheney and his aides met at least six times with Lay and other Enron officials while preparing the group's report, which provided the basis for the administration's energy policy proposals. Additionally, Cheney's staff met with an Enron-sponsored lobbying organization, the Clean Power Group.

Cheney claimed this access gave Enron no advantage. "The fact is Enron didn't get any special deals," he declared when questioned in January 2002. Yet an Enron memo discovered after that interview suggested the corporation shaped substantial portions of the task force's recommendations. When Cheney and Lay met in April 2001, Lay handed Cheney a three-page "wish list" of corporate recommendations. Representative Henry Waxman, the ranking minority member of the House Committee on Government Reform, ordered an analysis of the memo against the final report of the task force; it shows that the Cheney-led group adopted all or significant portions of the recommendations in seven of eight policy areas. Included were seventeen policies sought by Enron or that clearly benefited the company—among them proposals to extend federal control of transmission lines, use federal eminent domain authority to override state decisions on transmission line siting, expedite permission for new energy facilities, and limit the use of price controls. Noting that "there is no company in the country that stood to gain as much from the White House plan as Enron," Waxman wrote Cheney, "The recent revelations regarding the extent of Enron's contacts with the White House energy task force have only underscored the need for full public disclosure."

Under the Federal Advisory Committee Act of 1972, task forces like Cheney's must conduct public meetings, allow interested parties to attend, and keep publicly available records. But arguing "executive privilege," Cheney, his aides, and cabinet departments have continued to battle requests for records, despite legal challenges from the General Accounting Office (GAO) and private groups. One lawsuit freed up Energy Department documents that began to hint at the extent of the influence that energy corporations exercised over administration policies, but Cheney continued to stonewall.

The energy task force's recommendations were not the only benefits Enron got from Cheney; the vice president provided a number of other official services to the troubled corporation. Copies of e-mails obtained by the *New York Daily News* indicate that Cheney aided an attempt by Enron to force the Maharashtra State Electricity Board in India to pay it at least $2.3 billion in connection with a failed $2.9 billion plan to develop a power plant. A June 28, 2001, e-mail from a National Security Council aide read, "Good news is that the veep mentioned Enron in his meeting with [Indian Congress Party leader] Sonia Gandhi yesterday." Shortly after the September 11, 2001, terrorist attacks on the World Trade Center and the Pentagon, Cheney held a highly sensitive conversation with the foreign minister of India, whose country, a nuclear power, was concerned about the Bush administration's determination to work closely with the government of Pakistan, a neighboring country with which India had a long history of sour relations. Despite the high stakes for the administration's just announced war on terrorism, Cheney found time in that October 3, 2001, discussion to raise the power plant payment issue again. And when Cheney's energy task force was finalizing its report in August 2001, a draft document was altered to include a provision recommending that the U.S. secretaries of state and energy work with India to help that country maximize its domestic oil and gas production. "The energy plan does not discuss this recommendation or explain why maximizing oil and gas production in India should be a US national energy priority," Waxman wrote in a letter to Cheney. Instead, Waxman argued, the provision "benefited Enron by formally enlisting two Cabinet secretaries in Enron's conflict with the Indian government."

With the notable exception of Waxman, the Enron-Cheney connection garnered troublingly limited attention from congressional Democrats. Senator Joseph Lieberman announced that a committee he headed at the time would issue more than two dozen subpoenas that could cast light on Enron–White House contacts, but Lieberman's determination to maintain a "bipartisan" approach limited the scope of the inquiry. Despite the fact that they controlled the Senate, Democratic leaders appeared to be reluctant to invite charges that they were repaying the GOP for eight years of investigations into the Clinton administration. Many Democrats also worried that opening a more serious discussion of Enron would open them to scrutiny.

Cheney's refusal to cooperate with investigators—which presidential historian Stanley Kutler referred to as part of a broad "assault on the legal and Constitutional order" by the Bush administration—made a powerful case for the appointment of a special counsel to review the matter. Congress allowed the independent counsel law to expire in 1999, ceding to the attorney general the right to make such appointments. Attorney General John Ashcroft recused himself from Enron-related discussions, however, after it was learned that he had taken campaign contributions from Enron. But his aides remained free to make the call. John Conyers Jr., the ranking Democrat on the House Judiciary Committee, wrote the Justice Department in January 2002 to argue, "The Enron case represents one of the largest corporate frauds in the nation's history, and the potential for conflicts of interest is so sweeping that it necessitates an outside counsel to insure public confidence." Unfortunately, Conyers's call was little noted beyond the ranks of serious reformers like California representative Bob Filner, whose "sense of Congress" call for a special counsel made no progress in the Republican-controlled House of Representatives.

Conyers and Filner recognized the reality that a serious conflict-of-interest issue had arisen. Yet neither the Justice Department nor Congress was prepared to conduct the sort of investigation required to expose the full extent of the Bush administration's service to Enron. That investigation would have needed to be broad, since the connections with Enron were not limited to Cheney's office. From Secretary of the Army Thomas White, a former Enron executive, to U.S. trade representative Robert Zoellick, formerly on Enron's advisory council, Enron's tentacles had stretched throughout the Bush White House, shaping tax, trade, energy, and environmental policies. All of those connections and conflicts were worthy of legal and congressional scrutiny. But the place to begin the investigation was at Dick Cheney's door. If there was any realistic hope of exposing the extent to which Enron's machinations corrupted U.S. policy at home and abroad, then the office of the vice president was not only a good place to start, it was the essential beginning point.

ney and White House political czar Karl Rove, who appreciates the value of a vice president who is popular with the hard-liners, have made it their special responsibility to nurture relationships with the religious Right. Cheney is a regular on the social conservative banquet circuit, where he reassures the faithful that the administration is going to appoint judges who will not be afraid to legislate from the bench on issues such as abortion and prayer in the schools. He started off 2004, for instance, by revving up the troops at the Conservative Political Action Committee summit in Washington, along with speakers from the Christian Coalition, the Traditional Values Coalition, Phyllis Schlafly's Eagle Forum, Concerned Women of America, and the Family Research Council. Cheney works hard to do what Reverend Jerry Falwell in 2000 identified as the former defense secretary's primary political role: energizing the conservative base. Cheney and Rove are obsessed with the fact that, despite their best efforts, an estimated four million Christian fundamentalists failed to vote in the 2000 presidential election. They recognize the importance of judicial nomination fights as part of the strategy for energizing potential voters who tend to see politics as a dirty game but might be drawn into the process by the promise that their votes could ensure the recriminalization of abortion. That's why they have no qualms about advancing the nominations of extremists who frighten even Republican moderates in the Senate. When the Senate Judiciary Committee Democrats balk at a nominee, all the better. Cheney has since his days in the House operated on the theory that, as he states it, "confrontation fits our strategy. Polarization often has very beneficial results. If everything is handled through compromise and conciliation, if there are no real issues dividing us from the Democrats, why should the country [elect Republicans]."

In what may well be the most politicized White House in history, Cheney's office—where the staff of more than sixty aides far exceeds that of his predecessor, Al Gore—serves as the political nerve center. Rove, an able and aggressive strategist, is officially in charge of politics for the White House. But for all practical purposes, he reports to Dick Cheney, who once said, "I set out to be a political science teacher. My years in Washington sort of got in the way of that, but it all ties in. What I want to do is political stuff." In the current White House, it is Cheney, not Rove, who makes the most important connections between the "political stuff" and policy decisions. Cheney is quick to take charge of controversial initiatives involving everything from energy policy to homeland security and corporate reform. Often, Cheney takes on so many responsibilities that he botches the basics. In the early months of the administration, after a commission headed by former senators Warren Rudman and Gary Hart submitted a report calling for stepped-up counterterrorism measures, Cheney feared that Congress might get credit for taking the lead on national security. That would not do, because Cheney and Rove believe defense of the homeland is a "branded" Republican issue. So Cheney set up his own task force to make its own recommendations. As writer Joshua Micah Marshall noted, "Cheney's security task force did nothing for four months, lurching into action only after terrorists actually attacked America on September 11."

But Cheney was not chastened. As he has since the beginning of the transition period, he continues not merely to insert himself in every major debate within the administration, but to dominate them. Invariably, this means that ideology and politics trump open debate and the public good. In cabinet meetings and smaller strategy sessions, Cheney often plays a role similar to that of commissar in the former Soviet Union, inserting a political calculation into every dialogue. Ousted Treasury secretary Paul O'Neill, who had joined the administration at the behest of the vice president, described a classic Cheney intervention during a late 2002 internal debate about whether to propose a second round of tax cuts for wealthy Americans. O'Neill expressed concerns about mounting deficits, to which Cheney replied, "We won the midterm elections. This is our due." O'Neill, initially shocked by his old friend's "don't confuse me with the facts" absolutism, came to the conclusion that, far from being the balanced moderating force that press clips still sometimes suggested, Cheney had embraced "brazen ideology" that was "not penetrable by facts." O'Neill had no luck appealing to the obviously disengaged president, who seemed to the former Alcoa executive to be "like a blind man in a roomful of deaf people." After he left the cabinet, O'Neill explained to journalist Ron Suskind that "Cheney and a handful of others had become 'a Praetorian guard' that encircled the President. In terms of bringing new, transforming ideas to the Oval Office, 'this store was closed.' "

An earlier exile from Cheney's vast dominions, John DiIulio, who had headed the administration's Faith-Based Initiative, left the White House with similar concerns about the warping of policy for political purposes. "There is no precedent in any modern White House for what is going on in this one: a complete lack of a policy apparatus. What you've got is everything—and I mean everything—being run by the political arm. It's the reign of the Mayberry Machiavellis," said DiIulio. The White House, DiIulio argued in a remarkable January 2003 letter to *Esquire* magazine, "lacked even the most basic policy apparatus." DiIulio explained that when White House aides did start talking about a serious issue, it was not uncommon to witness "near instant shifts from discussing any actual policy pros and cons to discussing political communications, media strategy, et cetera."

It might appear, on the surface, that there would be a disconnect between the "brazen ideology" that so distressed O'Neill and the overarching "political arm" that troubled DiIulio. After all, wouldn't there be times when it made sense to back off a purist position in order to achieve electoral advantage? Of course, that's true, but this is where Cheney, the "to the right of . . . Genghis Khan" conservative who worked so hard to beat Ronald Reagan in 1976, comes in. At the heart of Cheney's calculus, whether the issue is energy policy, a judicial nomination, or war with Iraq, is a complex determination to exercise power with the purpose of attaining more power.

There is no question that Cheney is a true-blue conservative. Nor is there any question that, left to his own devices, he will veer far to the right of the political mainstream, as his congressional voting record well illustrates. But from the start of his career, Cheney has displayed a fierce aversion to sacrificing power for principle. The challenge that Cheney sets for himself is the balancing of the two demands. Thus, when Cheney steers the White House to the right, it is not merely to achieve an ideological goal; he also wants to make sure that there is a political payoff. So it was that while Cheney really did want another round of tax cuts to reward the Republican Party's contributor base, he did not push it until the Republicans had prevailed in the 2002 midterm elections. Another form of political calculus was in play when Cheney and Rove promoted the nomination of Mississippi federal judge Charles Pickering, whose history of opposing interracial marriage and defending cross burning did not sit well with civil rights activists, to the Fifth Circuit U.S. Court of Appeals, the circuit that traditionally has been relied upon to enforce civil rights laws in the Deep South. When the Senate

Judiciary Committee blocked Pickering's nomination in March 2002, the Cheney-Rove axis geared up to spin the decision as an affront to southern heritage and values. The goal was never in debate: get southern whites, especially men, stirred up enough to turn out in high numbers for Republicans seeking House and Senate seats.

The strategies that Cheney and Rove put in place worked well in southern states like Mississippi and Georgia, where Republicans had a very good year in 2002. But as that fall election approached, there was at least one state where the best-laid political plans of Dick Cheney seemed to be going awry.

Cheney likes his Democrats spineless. Along with other members of the administration, he was amused, and delighted as the 2002 elections approached, by the willingness of Senate majority leader Tom Daschle and House minority leader Dick Gephardt to sign on with White House legislative initiatives on everything from education to bankruptcy reform to war with Iraq. But not all Democrats were alike. And one senator, Minnesota's Paul Wellstone, seemed at every turn to be taking on the administration. Cheney had nurtured a deep disdain for Wellstone ever since the former college professor arrived in Washington in 1991, after upsetting an incumbent Republican senator. One of Wellstone's first acts in the Senate was to oppose the resolution authorizing the first President Bush to go to war with Iraq. Father Bush had uttered an obscenity when Wellstone raised the issue of the war with him back in 1991, and Cheney continued to agree with his former boss's assessment of the populist senator from the upper Midwest.

Of all Cheney's political projects in 2002, none was more high-profile, and more ham-handed, than his campaign to oust

Wellstone. The Minnesota race was critical. Democrats had only a one-seat majority in the Senate, and if Wellstone could be beaten, Cheney would, as vice president, be able to break tie votes in favor of the Republican agenda. Cheney decided that if only one Democrat went, it would be Wellstone.

How serious was the vice president about getting rid of Wellstone? So serious that he got very personally and very publicly involved in the selection of the Republican nominee to oppose the senator. But wait a minute, aren't the Republicans of Minnesota supposed to choose their Senate candidates? Not in Dick Cheney's political world. That's what Tim Pawlenty, the majority leader of the Minnesota House of Representatives, learned on April 18, 2001. A popular Republican, Pawlenty had decided to try to challenge Wellstone. Pawlenty would have to face St. Paul mayor Norm Coleman, a party-switching former Democrat who had chaired the campaign for the Bush-Cheney ticket when it lost Minnesota in 2000, in the party primary. But he felt confident about his prospects until he got the call. Ninety minutes before the press conference where he was scheduled to announce his candidacy, the phone in Pawlenty's car rang. It was Vice President Dick Cheney calling with some advice. If Pawlenty knew what was good for him politically, he wouldn't go ahead with the announcement. The White House had decided that Coleman was going to be the candidate against Wellstone, and Cheney made it abundantly clear that he did not want Coleman to face a primary challenge from a credible Republican.

Pawlenty was dumbfounded. But he was also a loyal Republican. "When you get a call from the vice president of the United States, who indicates that he's speaking on behalf of the president, that's something I respect and honor," said Pawlenty, who shocked even his own supporters when he dutifully declared at that day's press conference that he would not upset the Coleman juggernaut.

Unfortunately for Cheney, whose uncanny ability to pick a loser was by now well established, Coleman didn't quite cut it as a candidate. With huge infusions of campaign cash and regular visits to the state by Cheney and Bush, Coleman was able to hold his own against Wellstone into September. But a funny thing happened in early October, when the Senate voted on a resolution authorizing the administration to wage war against Iraq. The White House political operation had pressed for a war vote before the election in order to ramp up patriotic sentiments that had been running high since the September 11, 2001, terrorist attacks on the World Trade Center and the Pentagon. The plan was to put Democrats in the Senate on the spot. Most of them buckled. In fact, all but one of the Democratic senators who were in competitive races around the country in 2002 supported the resolution, which passed by a wide margin. The one exception was Wellstone, who said the administration had not made the case for war. In an interview at the time of the vote, Wellstone said he was not going to let Bush and Cheney back him into a corner. He knew the political risks; he was even told by one Democratic senator that he had ruined his chances for reelection. But Wellstone was confident. He had faith in the people of Minnesota, he said: "They're not going to let Bush and Cheney tell them who to elect."

Wellstone's confidence was well-placed. After his vote against the war, he began to open up a commanding lead over Coleman. It was clear he was going to win, and there was nothing Dick Cheney could do about it. Then, less than two weeks before the election, Wellstone was killed in a plane crash in northern Minnesota.

Wellstone's wife and daughter were killed as well, along with several campaign aides and two pilots. It was a devastating blow for the senator's two sons. The administration, which had worked so hard to defeat Wellstone, added one final bit of insult to injury. When the date for Wellstone's memorial service was set, word came from the White House that a high-ranking member of the administration would attend: Vice President Dick Cheney. It seemed an astute political move. There was a great deal of anger in Minnesota over the White House's treatment of Wellstone. By attending the memorial service, Cheney could make it seem as if it had all just been "political stuff." Bygones would be bygones.

Within hours, however, it was announced that Cheney would not be making the trip to Minnesota. The White House attempted to spin the story, suggesting that traffic and Secret Service concerns had been a factor. But the truth finally came out. The Wellstone family had informed the White House that Cheney, who had spent a year trying to defeat the senator, was not welcome. White House aides were shocked. They had little experience of someone saying no to Cheney. He was "the boss," the commissar, the CEO, the prime minister—effectively, the president. He had the run of the White House, a place in every debate, control of every portfolio that interested him. But Dick Cheney had met his match in the sons of the senator he had so despised. The vice president might have the power to crash any meeting in the White House. But he was not going to crash Paul Wellstone's memorial service.

CHAPTER 8

DICK CHENEY'S WAR

Richard Clarke: "The vice president started attending meetings."
Chris Matthews: "Did he tip the scales?"
Richard Clarke: "Of course."
Chris Matthews: "Did he have his thumb on the scales?"
Richard Clarke: "Look, the vice president was in meetings that vice presidents have never been in before, helping shape the policy before it got to the president."
—MSNBC *Hardball* exchange, March 31, 2004, regarding Iraq war planning within the Bush administration

[Clarke] wasn't in the loop, frankly, on a lot of this stuff.
—Dick Cheney, March 23, 2004, appearing on Rush Limbaugh's radio show to counter Clarke's charges

That is, frankly, a lie.
—*Atlanta Journal-Constitution* editorial, March 24, 2004

During the 2000 presidential campaign, George W. Bush's handlers worried whenever he was questioned about foreign affairs. Bush, whose passport remained remarkably unblemished by the stamps of foreign lands, had never taken an interest in the rest of

STEFAN ZAKLIN/GETTY IMAGES

Three strikes: On the eve of war with Iraq, Cheney told NBC's Tim Russert, "We know [Saddam Hussein] has reconstituted these [chemical weapons] programs. We know he's out trying once again to produce nuclear weapons, and we know that he has a long-standing relationship with various terrorist groups, including the al-Qaeda organization." (2003: Rumsfeld, Cheney, and Acting Army Secretary Les Brownlee)

the world. And it showed. While campaigning in New Hampshire, the candidate sat down with the political reporter for a Boston television station, who without informing the campaign had prepared an international affairs "pop quiz" for the candidate. Bush aides cringed as the man they were proposing to place in charge of the most powerful nation on the planet struggled to identify the leaders of world hot spots. "Can you name the general who is in charge of Pakistan?" asked reporter Andy Hiller.

"The new Pakistani general, he's just been elected—not elected, this guy took over office. It appears this guy is going to bring stability to the country, and I think that's good news for the subcontinent."

Yes, but what is his name?

It was painful to watch Bush struggling. "General, er, uh . . ."

Next question.

How about India, another nuclear power? "The new prime minister of India is . . ." Bush shook his head. "No," he did not know that guy's name, either. What about the leader of Taiwan, a country the United States was pledged to defend against all threats? "No." Chechnya, which was degenerating into one of the most dangerous places on the planet? "No."

That was the end of Hiller's list of questions. Bush's score, as reported broadly in the following days, was an "F". Bush spokeswoman Karen Hughes was in full damage control mode. "The person who is running for president is seeking to be the leader of the free world, not a *Jeopardy!* contestant," she declared, adding that "99.9 percent of Americans" didn't know the name of the president of Chechnya. But for all the bravado, Bush campaign insiders continued to fret about their inability to get the candidate to wrap his mind around the world. Even after months of briefings, counseling sessions, and introductions to maps—many of which had been overseen by Dick Cheney—there was still a great deal of concern any time Bush attempted to address foreign policy. He kept referring to Greeks as "Grecians," to Kosovars as "Kosovarians," to the East Timorese as "East Timorians." And he kept confusing countries, mixing up places like Slovakia and Slovenia, which both started with "S" but which had very different relationships with the United States.

The approach of Bush's three October debates with Democrat Al Gore, who had been the point man for the Clinton administration on a number of international fronts, was a cause for heightened blood pressure rates among Bush's aides. But the candidate managed to make it through the debates relatively unscarred. Indeed, he surprised even some of his critics by delivering a reasonably nuanced answer to a question about the deployment of U.S. troops abroad. While it was known that many of his aides and counselors—including Cheney, Wolfowitz, and Rumsfeld—had embraced the expansionist gospel of U.S. engagement with the world that was preached by the neoconservative movement's shadowy Project for the New American Century, Bush did not exactly sound like a military adventurer. While the Project for the New American Century had dispatched a January 1998 letter to President Clinton calling for shifting policy toward Iraq to achieve the express goal of "the removal of Saddam Hussein's regime from power," Bush didn't sound like a "regime-change" kind of guy. Referring to Gore, Bush said, "The vice president and I have a disagreement about the use of troops. He believes in nation building. I would be very careful about using our troops as nation builders," adding that "I don't want to try to put our troops in all places at all times. I don't want to be the world's policeman."

When Gore started going on about how the United States needed to step up to its leadership responsibilities in this "unique period in world history," Bush jumped in to say, "I'm not so sure the role of the United States is to go around the world and say, 'This is the way it's gonna be.' " Sounding more like Senator Robert Byrd, the white-haired prophet from West Virginia who thundered warnings from the well of the Senate against the folly of imperial arrogance, than another of the boys at the Project for the New American Century, Bush declared, "I just don't think it's the role of the United States to walk into a country and say, 'We do it this way; so should you.' " Some Americans who listened to Bush might have imagined, if they were of a particularly optimistic bent, that this was a candidate who was going to make the United States a responsible player in the world, a country that accepted differences among peoples, that preferred pragmatism over crusades, and that would act on the global stage only in cooperation with other nations. Certainly they would not have presumed that in less than two and a half years, Bush would, without the support of the United Nations or traditional allies in Europe, lead the United States into a preemptive war against another land, with the goal not of defending America, but of forcing "regime change."

The problem was that Americans who listened to George W. Bush in any of his three debates were paying attention to the wrong end of the Republican ticket. The debate that Americans should have been glued to was the single clash between Democratic vice presidential candidate Joe Lieberman and Republican Dick Cheney. Facing off against each other on the campus of a small college in Kentucky, the vice presidential candidates conducted a civilized debate that was hailed by just about everyone who watched as the most substantive of the season. These fellows, though they did not disagree on all that much, seemed to be saying things that mattered. That was especially true of Cheney when the subject of "responsibilities" around the world came up. Generally, he wanted it known that under his watch, U.S. troops would deploy around the planet as "warriors" rather than as peacekeepers. And, of course, he repeated his by now tired argument against the peace dividend, complaining that under Bill Clinton's leadership, "we have seen a reduction of our forces far beyond anything that was justified by the end of the cold war."

But where Cheney really got going was on the subject of Iraq.

When moderator Bernard Shaw asked Cheney whether he would support a "deadly policy" if Iraqi president Saddam Hussein was found to be developing weapons of mass destruction, the Republican candidate replied ominously, "We might have no other choice." Then Cheney began, as was his tendency, to lecture about how the Middle East had gone to hell in a handbasket since he had given up the keys to the Pentagon. "The thing about Iraq, of course, was at the end of the war, we had pretty well decimated their military. We had put them back in a box, so to speak. We had a strong international coalition raid against them, effective economic sanctions, and a very robust inspection regime that was in place, so that the inspection regime, under UN auspices, was able to do a good job of stripping out the capacity to build weapons of mass destruction, the work that (Saddam had) been doing that had not been destroyed during the war, and biological chemical agents as well as a nuclear program," Cheney grumbled. "Unfortunately, now we find ourselves in a situation where that started to fray on us, where the coalition now no longer is tied tightly together. Recently the United Arab Emirates and Bahrain, two Gulf states, have reopened diplomatic relations with Baghdad. The Russians and the French now are flying commercial airliners back into Baghdad and, sort of, thumbing their nose, if you will, at the international sanctions regime. And, of course, the UN inspectors have been kicked out, and there's been absolutely no response. So we're in a situation today where I think our posture vis-à-vis Iraq is weaker than it was at the end of the war."

That was a mighty debatable point. Seven years of United Nations weapons inspections had, by any honest measure, been a stunning success. Indeed, Scott Ritter, a senior American member of the UN weapons inspection team that had scoured Iraq for WMDs in the 1990s, said, "I bear personal witness through seven years as a chief weapons inspector in Iraq for the United Nations to both the scope of Iraq's weapons of mass destruction programs and the effectiveness of UN weapons inspectors in ultimately eliminating them." U.S. senator Bob Graham, the Democrat from Florida who served as the ranking minority member of the Senate Intelligence Committee before the 2000 election and chairman of the committee after Democrats regained control of the Senate in 2001, said that as someone who had read all the reports regarding Iraqi WMDs during the 1990s, he had not seen evidence that the threat level had increased, as Cheney claimed. In fact, most serious observers thought Iraq was a basket-case country that posed little serious threat even to its neighbors. Iraq was so toothless, in fact, that many of the world's top corporations, including Cheney's Halliburton, had been doing business with Saddam for a number of years. Yet there was Dick Cheney, gravely expressing his concern that "if, in fact, Saddam Hussein were taking steps to try to rebuild nuclear capability or weapons of mass destruction, we'd have to give very serious consideration to military action to stop that activity." The candidate closed his soliloquy, one of the longest statements of a long debate, by raising an eyebrow and saying, "I don't think you can afford to have a man like Saddam Hussein with nuclear weapons, say, in the Middle East."

In just one more reminder of why he was perhaps the worst choice Democrats could have found to put up against Cheney, Joe Lieberman did not begin to question the Republican candidate's "five minutes to midnight" fearmongering. Lieberman, one of the most hawkish Democrats in the Senate and a faithful follower of the neoconservative dogmas that Cheney preached, actually sided with his opponent. Noting that "Al Gore and I were two of the ten Democrats in the Senate who crossed party lines to support President Bush and Secretary Cheney in (the first Gulf) war," Lieberman agreed that "we will not enjoy real stability in the Middle East until Saddam Hussein is gone."

With that, Bernie Shaw shifted the questioning, making one of those casual leaps that said everything about the lens through which the debate over Iraq was frequently viewed: his next questions were about energy policy. "Many experts," he noted, "are forecasting continuing chaotic oil prices on the world market."

As it happened, Shaw was not alone in linking the fact that Iraq sat above some of the world's largest reserves of crude oil to the debate over energy policy. Just three months later, it was on Dick Cheney's mind. Now working out of the White House, he began to formulate a new energy policy for the United States. Cheney did not actually mention that his energy task force would be discussing Iraq. But when a court finally ordered the Commerce Department to turn over records that the conservative watchdog group Judicial Watch had sued for under the

Freedom of Information Act, three documents stood out. There was a map of Iraqi oil fields, pipelines, refineries, and terminals. And there were two charts listing Iraqi oil and gas projects and "Foreign Suitors for Iraqi Oilfield Contracts." That Cheney saw Iraq—or, more specifically, the current government of Iraq—as an energy policy issue was no secret. In the most wildly over-the-top speech delivered by any of the administration's top officials during the debate prior to the 2002 congressional vote on whether to authorize the invasion of that country, Cheney informed the Veterans of Foreign Wars (VFW) national convention in Nashville, Tennessee, that this would, in fact, be a war for oil. After asserting that Saddam had "resumed his efforts to acquire nuclear weapons," Cheney told the veterans, "Armed with an arsenal of these weapons of terror, and seated atop 10 percent of the world's oil reserves, Saddam Hussein could then be expected to seek domination of the entire Middle East, take control of the world's energy supplies, directly threaten America's friends throughout the region, and subject the United States or any other nation to nuclear blackmail."

It was an apocalyptic vision, especially for a man who had wed himself to an American oil industry that had grown fat and comfortable because of the ability of the United States government to play one oil-rich country, or region, against another. And though Cheney's doom-and-gloom scenario would prove to be unrealistic, his ability to act upon the fears that he had stirred was very real indeed.

But neither the politics of oil nor the economics of the oil industry to which he and George W. Bush had sworn their blood oaths could begin to explain Dick Cheney's passion for war with Iraq.

For Cheney, Iraq was much more than an attractive source of revenue for firms such as Halliburton. Removing Saddam Hussein had been a personal project of long standing for the vice president. And it was difficult to tell anymore where exactly the lines were drawn between oil and vengeance, politics and ideology, fact and fiction. There was, however, no question that, as journalist Bob Woodward would suggest in *Plan of Attack* (2004), his book-length examination of the administration's preparations to invade Iraq in the spring of 2003, Cheney was a "powerful steamrolling force" advocating for war.

Nor was there any doubt that Cheney had the ability to steer the president and the rest of the administration—which the vice president had seeded with his neoconservative allies—in the direction he chose. As writer James Mann would note in *Rise of the Vulcans,* "The selection of Cheney was of surpassing importance for the future direction of foreign policy. It went further than any other single decision Bush made toward determining the nature and the policies of the administration he would lead." *Weekly Standard* editor William Kristol would put it more succinctly: "When Cheney talks, it's Bush." And on the subject of Iraq, the usually circumspect Cheney seemed to be talking all the time.

Cheney's obsession with Iraq had roots going back at least to Operation Scorpion, his Pentagon office's ill-fated "don't tell Powell or anybody else" scheme to invade Iraq and eliminate Saddam Hussein as part of the first Gulf War in 1991. During the wilderness years of the 1990s, Cheney had not been above doing a little Halliburton business with Iraq. But the former secretary of defense let it be known that, had it been left to him, Saddam would have been long gone. Even as the Clinton administration regularly dispatched planes to bomb Iraq and battled within the United Nations to maintain draconian economic sanctions, Cheney griped that the Democrats were letting Saddam get out of "the box" that the 1991 Gulf War had constructed for him. When a motley crew of Iran-contra schemers, former Dan Quayle staffers, and assorted hangers-on from Cheney's Pentagon cobbled together the Project for the New American Century as the defense and foreign policy arm of the neoconservative movement in 1997, Cheney was quick to make common cause with the Iraq-obsessed partisans who, in the words of a May 2004 *Vanity Fair* article on their endeavor, had made the removal of Saddam "a kind of panacea for all the Middle East's ills and a solution for dealing with the rise of Islamic terror and bringing democracy to Iraq and the Middle East."

When he was pulling together the new Bush administration in the winter of 2000–2001, Cheney had been meticulous about establishing what Paul O'Neill would describe—echoing Robert Hartmann, a Cheney critic from the Ford administration— as a "Praetorian guard" of true believers. The Cheney-forged White House became the Project for the New American Century's job center. Rumsfeld was running the Pentagon, along with Douglas Feith, an old comrade who was brought back to serve as undersecretary of defense for policy. They were backed up by William Luti, a former Newt Gingrich aide who was now in charge of Department of Defense military policy regarding the Middle East. Wolfowitz set up a foreign policy shop within the Pentagon in order to undermine Colin Powell, who, as in the first Gulf War, kept asking difficult questions about evidence and justifications and endgames. Stephen Hadley, an ally from the first Bush term, was added to National Security Adviser Condoleezza

Rice's staff. Scooter Libby, who had rewritten the controversial 1992 Defense Planning Guidance document that had been a precursor to the neocon adventure, was right next to Cheney, serving as chief of staff in the vice presidential office that was rapidly becoming a kind of clubhouse for the new administration's howl-at-the-moon crowd.

There was always some debate about whether Cheney was a real neoconservative or simply an old-school cold warrior who had found new enemies for the twenty-first century. But there was no question that Cheney was, if not a member of the neocon cell, a trusted fellow traveler. He even distributed the movement's magazine, sending out an aide to pick up stacks of the *Weekly Standard,* which was edited by Project for the New American Century principal William Kristol, for distribution in the White House. Cheney was so with the program that some White House aides suggested he was a truer believer than some of the preeminent neoconservatives.

Ten days after the new administration took office, at the first National Security Council meeting, it became clear to Secretary of the Treasury Paul O'Neill that Cheney and other hard-liners "were already planning the next war in Iraq and the shape of a post-Saddam country." In fact, O'Neill noted, the usually quiet and unrevealing Cheney displayed "uncharacteristic excitement" when George Tenet rolled out a tablecloth-size aerial photo that the CIA director said might show "a plant that produces either chemical or biological materials for weapons manufacture." O'Neill suggested that the picture of a factory looked like a lot of other factories around the world and asked, "What makes us suspect that this one is producing chemical or biological weapons?" Tenet admitted that there was "no confirming intelligence," which deflated the partylike atmosphere. But, noted Ron Suskind, who recounted O'Neill's experience in *The Price of Loyalty* (2004), "Ten days in, and it was about Iraq."

For Cheney, it would always be about Iraq. The man had what administration aides described to Bob Woodward as a "fever" for "regime change." According to Woodward, Cheney kept Iraq on a "low boil" through the first eight months of the new administration. Even as Cheney was busy setting up his energy and antiterrorism task forces early in 2001, he and Rumsfeld always seemed to be circulating memos with titles like "Plan for Post-Saddam Iraq" or the March 5, 2001, document titled "Foreign Suitors for Iraqi Oilfield Contracts," which started at the Pentagon and ended up in the paperwork for the energy task force.

Yet if it was a neoconservative article of faith that Saddam would eventually become a target, it was also a basic tenet of the movement that it would take something big to convince Congress of the necessity to attack Iraq. The Project for the New American Century's 2000 working paper titled "Rebuilding America's Defenses: Strategy, Forces and Resources for a New Century" had explained that those who were out to target Iraq would probably have to wait for a "catastrophic and catalyzing event—like a new Pearl Harbor."

It would not be a long wait. Eight months into the new administration, nineteen followers of Osama bin Laden, a millionaire Saudi Arabian who despised Saddam almost as much as he did America, flew jet planes into the World Trade Center buildings and the Pentagon on September 11, 2001. Cheney was in the White House on the day of the attack. When White House counterterrorism czar Richard Clarke proposed the first elements of a response to the crisis, it was Cheney who yelled, "Do it." Later, when Clarke called the Presidential Emergency Operations Center, the East Wing bunker where Cheney had relocated, Clarke wrote, "The person answering the line grunted and passed the phone to [army] Major [Mike] Fenzel. 'Who's the asshole answering the phone for you, Mike?' I asked. 'That would be the vice president, Dick.' "

Cheney was answering phones, barking out orders, and taking charge, just as he had trained to do two decades earlier when the Reagan administration had secretly identified Cheney and Rumsfeld to lead "continuity of government teams" in preparation for a nuclear attack. Cheney was in charge on September 11 and in the days that immediately followed the attack. Indeed, he was such a dominant player that White House aides became concerned that the president's secondary status had been exposed. As Julian Borger wrote in London's *Guardian* newspaper on January 12, 2004, "After perceptions spread early in the administration that Vice President Dick Cheney and the Republicans' political mastermind, Karl Rove, were really making policy, the White House publicity machine dedicated itself to building Mr. Bush up as a decisive leader. Presidential aides have 'leaked' anecdotes to the press showing Mr. Bush making tough decisions. In Bob Woodward's book *Bush at War* (2002), based principally on the celebrated Washington journalist's interviews with the president and top officials, there is no doubt who is in charge as the nation faces its greatest challenge since Pearl Harbor."

It would not be long, however, before Cheney would emerge from the "secure undisclosed location" to which he was consigned and, in Borger's words, renew suspicions that America's fate was in the hands of "an administration nominally led by a disengaged figurehead president but driven by a 'praetorian guard' of hardline rightwingers led by Vice President Dick Cheney, ready to bend circumstances and facts to fit their political agenda."

The facts that would most need bending in the months to come had to do with Iraq. When the cabinet met on September 15, 2001, at Camp David, the neoconservatives were so hyped about Iraq that, according to an account of the preparations for war published in the May 2004 edition of *Vanity Fair,* "during the lunch break, the president sent a message to Wolfowitz and the other neocons that he did not wish to hear any more about Iraq that day."

The target after September 11 was going to be al-Qaeda, bin Laden's terrorist network, not Iraq. Indeed, if the United States was attacking anywhere, it would be in Afghanistan, where the fundamentalist Taliban government had provided refuge for al-Qaeda. That was fine by Cheney. The vice president was not so obsessed with Iraq that he would neglect an obvious target of the administration's newly declared war on terrorism. But he was obsessed enough to begin mounting a campaign to tie al-Qaeda to Iraq. It was going to be a tough connection to make. Osama bin Laden and his followers hated Saddam Hussein, a secularist whose government included Christians and women, and Saddam feared the fanatical religionists as he did all movements that might organize opposition to his oppressive regime.

But Cheney was determined. He became a regular visitor to the CIA, where, the vice president would later explain, he made it his business to "ask a hell of a lot of questions." Reportedly, one of the vice president's most frequently asked questions was "Why doesn't your intelligence support what we know is out there?"

When a CIA briefer did not provide him with the answers he desired, Cheney reportedly demanded that she be replaced. Congressman Silvestre Reyes, a Texas Democrat and member of the House Intelligence Committee, said in July 2003 that he knew of at least three intelligence analysts who felt pressured to warp their findings. So troubling were the reports of Cheney's repeated visits to the CIA headquarters, and of his badgering of analysts, that three members of the House Intelligence Committee finally dispatched a letter to the vice president that read, "These visits are unprecedented. Normally, vice presidents, yourself included, receive regular briefings from [the] CIA in your office and have a CIA officer on permanent detail. There is no reason for the vice president to make personal visits to the CIA."

When the CIA would not make the connections he wanted, Cheney started relying on information from an independent intelligence unit that Rumsfeld had set up inside the Pentagon. Cheney never turned, however, to the State Department's highly regarded Bureau of Intelligence and Research, known as INR, where analysts maintained the sort of healthy skepticism that allowed them to be far more consistently correct about Iraq than the CIA or the Pentagon. "One would think if Cheney was on some sort of noble pursuit of the truth and really wanted to get into details, he would have noticed that INR had very loud and lengthy dissents on some critical pieces of Iraq intelligence," explained Greg Thielmann, who served as director of strategic, proliferation, and military affairs in the INR. "You'd think he might want to hear from us. It never happened, of course, because Cheney wasn't engaged in an academic search for the truth."

That became obvious as the months after September 11

A Briefing Encounter

President Bush took a blow to his credibility when it was revealed that his January 28, 2003, State of the Union script included sixteen words that suggested that Iraq's Saddam Hussein had sought "significant quantities" of uranium from the African nation of Niger. The line was included in the speech to create the impression that Iraq was developing a nuclear threat that the United States needed to address.

The problem with the Iraq-Niger "connection" was that the CIA and the International Atomic Energy Agency had established that the documents on which the claim was based were crude forgeries. If that wasn't enough, a veteran U.S. diplomat had, almost a year earlier, traveled to Niger and established that the claim was "highly dubious."

But Bush was deliberately vague in making claims about Iraq and nuclear weapons compared with Dick Cheney. In August 2002, Cheney bluntly declared, "We know that Saddam has resumed his efforts to acquire nuclear weapons." Seven months later, Cheney was still peddling the claim. On NBC's *Meet the Press,* three days before the invasion of Iraq began, Cheney said of Iraqi leader Saddam Hussein, "[We] believe he has, in fact, re-constituted nuclear weapons."

Cheney, who made regular visits to the Central Intelligence Agency to badger analysts to come up with more "evidence" about Iraq's weapons of mass destruction, was always looking for a way to prove that Iraq was piecing together a nuclear program.

That's how he crossed paths with Ambassador Joe Wilson, a highly regarded U.S. diplomat who has served stints in both Iraq and Africa. To be precise, the vice president and the diplomat never actually talked to each other.

"The vice president likes to say, and has said repeatedly, 'I have never met Joe Wilson.' And I am equally delighted to say I have never met Dick Cheney," jokes Wilson.

But there is definitely a Cheney-Wilson connection. Indeed, theirs is a classic story of how intelligence gathering works when a member of the executive branch seeks "evidence" that intelligence professionals and diplomats say does not exist.

Wilson explains how their interaction began:

"What happens in the vice president's office—this happens generally at the senior level—is that you get regular briefings from the CIA briefers. They come down from the agency," says Wilson. "The briefer is a guy who assembles all the issues but is not an expert on any of the issues, and he comes down and briefs it. The vice president sits across from him."

Early in 2002, during one of the briefings, Cheney was again asking questions about Iraqi nukes. "On this particular day, the vice president said to him, 'Gee, what about this report of uranium from Niger? You don't have anything on that.' It's something as innocuous as that. That is taken by the briefer as a 'tasker.' The briefer goes back, and the bureaucracy, the $35 billion-a-year intelligence bureaucracy that reports to the president and the vice president of the United States, acts. Their way of acting in this [Iraq-Niger] case was to, among other things, call me in to ask what I knew about it and then, ultimately, ask me to go out and check it out. The vice president ultimately admitted that. He said, 'Oh, yeah, I raised this question with the briefer,' and then he said to Tim Russert that the briefer came back two days later and said, 'We don't have anything, boss.' "

That's where Wilson says things stopped making sense. "Now, I don't know about you, but if I'm running a $35 billion- or $40 billion-a-year corporation designed to provide me with information, I don't want the briefer to come back in two days and say, 'We don't have anything, boss.' And I think that, if anything, Dick Cheney is a hell of a lot more rigorous in the demands that he would put on the bureaucracy. So I don't believe that for a minute."

So what gives? How come Cheney, who supposedly was obsessed with proving that Iraq was reconstituting its nuclear program, requested information on Iraqi purchases of uranium from Niger and then suddenly lost interest?

The best explanation is that by claiming he let the issue die when the briefer dismissed it, Cheney could argue that he never read the report Wilson put together when he went to Niger. That way, Cheney could say he was not familiar with the conclusion Wilson reached in

February 2002: that the report of Iraq trying to obtain uranium from Niger was not credible.

Since Cheney was relying on the Iraq-Niger connection to help legitimize his fearmongering, he certainly wouldn't want to acknowledge that he was aware a senior diplomat discredited the "evidence" on which his statements were based.

Wilson does not buy Cheney's claim that he never saw the diplomat's report.

When Wilson got back from Niger, he says, "I submitted my report through the regular channels and it got circulated. There's a report out there."

And Wilson is sure Cheney saw it, or at least was briefed about it.

"If you are senior enough to ask the question, you are senior enough to get a very specific response," Wilson explains. "In addition to the circular report that was sent around as a consequence of my trip, I have every confidence that one way or another the vice president was directly briefed as well."

Bottom line: "I have a high level of confidence that the vice president got briefed and decided just to ignore the briefing," says Wilson.

When the controversy about Bush's State of the Union reference to the Iraq-Niger connection began to heat up in June 2003, word spread that "an unnamed diplomat" had "given a negative report" regarding the uranium claim almost a year before Bush delivered his fateful address. In July, Wilson outed himself as the "unnamed diplomat" in a *New York Times* op-ed piece that asked, "What else are they lying about?"

Within days, in what was read as an attempt to undermine Wilson's credibility, someone at the White House leaked to journalist Robert Novak details about the ambassador's wife, Valerie Plame, who was a CIA operative working on weapons of mass destruction issues.

The leak exposed Plame, who was working undercover at the time, to potential dangers and threatened to ruin her career. It also violated a 1982 federal law that prohibited revealing the identity of U.S. intelligence agents.

So who was responsible for the leak? Wilson's waiting for various investigations to help settle the issue.

"With respect to who actually leaked the information, there are really only a few people—far fewer than the president let on when he said there are a lot of senior administration officials—who could have done it," says Wilson. "At the end of the day, you have to have the means, the keys to the conversation at which somebody might drop my wife's name—deliberately or not—a national security clearance, and a reason to be talking about this.

"When you look at all of that, there are really very few people who exist at that nexis between national security and foreign policy and politics. You can count them, literally, on two hands," adds Wilson.

Is Dick Cheney one of those people?

In addition to several of Cheney's aides, Wilson says, "the vice president is one of those people."

wore on and Cheney became known for peddling outlandish claims that always seemed to circle back to the point that Iraq was, as Cheney would claim months after the war had begun, "the geographic base of the terrorists who have had us under assault for many years, but most especially on 9/11." Cheney became the tribune for crackpot conspiracy theories that had long since been discredited in the intelligence community. He suggested that Iraq might have played a role in the 1993 terrorist bombing of the World Trade Center. He spread the word that Mahomed Atta, one of the 9/11 hijackers, had met with an Iraqi intelligence agent in Prague. Each time Cheney trotted out a new complaint, the CIA or the FBI or a foreign intelligence agency would quietly explain that, no, what the vice president was saying was not credible. *New Yorker* writer Seymour Hersh wrote a detailed report in that magazine's October 27, 2003 issue on how Cheney had been duped by everyone from the neocons to Iraqi con man in chief Ahmad Chalabi. And it finally got so bad that, in a November 17, 2003 report titled "How Dick Cheney Sold the War: Why He Fell for Bad Intelligence and Pitched It to the President," *Newsweek* magazine noted, "A Cheney aide took strong exception to the notion that the vice president was at the receiving end of some kind of pipeline for half-baked or fraudulent intelligence, or that he was somehow carrying water for the neocons or anyone else's self-serving agendas."

The Cheney aide had a point. While the vice president was hardly expert in the matters at hand, it was a stretch to suggest that he was a dupe. After so many of his claims about al-Qaeda connections and WMDs had been discredited, Cheney's determination to keep pressing them suggests that he would be more accurately described as a propagandist. His desire for war with Iraq was now so fevered that he would warp just about any fact, skew just about any debate, and make just about any claim to advance the "case" for war. "What is it about Cheney's character and background that makes him such a Cassandra?" demanded *Time* magazine in its after-the-fact dissection of Cheney's repeated distortions. "And did his powerful dirge drown out more modulated voices in the councils of power in Washington and in effect launch America on the path to war?"

The answer to the latter question is, undoubtedly, "Yes."

But it was not an easy crusade for Cheney.

The vice president was frequently shot down when he attempted to pitch his theories about terrorist connections and weapons of mass destruction. That's what happened in March 2002, when he visited Middle Eastern capitals to try to drum up support for the war in what Cheney thought would be a reprise of the tarmac-to-tarmac diplomacy that built the coalition in favor of the 1991 Gulf War. Unfortunately for Cheney, the case he made was so unconvincing that, as *Washington Monthly* noted, "he returned a week later with the Arabs lining up behind Saddam and against us—a major embarrassment for the administration." But Cheney kept chugging. With the approach of the fall 2002 House and Senate votes on whether to authorize the use of force against Iraq, he popped up at the VFW national convention and simply declared, "There is no doubt that Saddam Hussein now has weapons of mass destruction."

Actually, there was a good deal of doubt. More than 150 members of the House and Senate voted against giving the administration the war authorization. And it appeared that their doubts were shared by at least one highly ranked member of the Bush cabinet. Secretary of State Colin Powell, who had challenged Cheney during the days leading up to the first Gulf War, was again skeptical. Powell and Cheney clashed frequently after the congressional vote. Powell wanted to work with the UN, Cheney wanted a war. When Powell prepared to address the United Nations on February 5, 2003, according to *Vanity Fair*'s re-creation of events, "Cheney's staff constantly pushed for certain intelligence on Iraq's alleged ties to terrorists to be included—including information that Powell and his people angrily insisted was not reliable."

Aware that Powell was balking, Cheney approached the secretary of state and said, "Your poll numbers are in the seventies. You can afford to lose a few points." Powell ended up losing more than just poll points. When he delivered a speech that attempted to balance his relative moderation with Cheney's extremism, the gathered diplomats were underwhelmed. Before Powell had left the building, it was clear that the speech had been a failure. The UN would not be on board. But there would still be a war.

Cheney had gotten Bush to sign off on that decision weeks, perhaps months, before. As Bob Woodward noted, Cheney was "just down the hall in the West Wing from the president," and he was "obsessed with Saddam and taking him out." Powell and others might raise questions, especially about the lack of a plan for what to do after the invasion, but it was a hopeless endeavor. "Like with a horse, Powell is always able to lead Bush to water," explained Delaware's senator Joe Biden, the ranking Democrat on the Senate Foreign Relations Committee. "But just as he is about to put his head down, Cheney up in the saddle says, 'Uh-uh,' and yanks the reins before Bush can drink the water. That's my image of how it goes."

That's just about right.

Richard Clarke, who left the White House out of frustration with Cheney's warping of policy on Iraq and the impact the vice president's actions had on the real war on terrorism, says there was never any question that Cheney used his unique status to tip the scales toward war. "Look," Clarke explained in an interview with Chris Matthews on MSNBC's *Hardball,* "the vice president was in meetings that vice presidents have never been in before, helping shape the policy before it got to the president."

Matthews then asked the question that mattered: "Had [Cheney] been against the war with Iraq, would we have gone?"

"I doubt it," Clarke replied. "He was critical."

Clarke was wrong in only one sense. Cheney was not "critical." He was, undoubtedly, "definitional."

In March 2003, on the eve of war, it would be Cheney, not Bush, who appeared on NBC's *Meet the Press* to make the final case for a decision that he had made years before. The United States was about to launch Operation Scorpion version 2.0. The time had come to implement a contemporary variation on Cheney's long-deferred plan for regime change in Iraq.

Cheney opened, as he typically did, with a lie. Asked by host Tim Russert if the decision had been made to go to war, he replied, "Well, I think we are still in the final stages of diplomacy, obviously."

The lies just kept on coming. Without prompting, Cheney said of Saddam Hussein, "We know he's reconstituted these [chemical weapons] programs. We know he's out trying once again to produce nuclear weapons, and we know that he has a long-standing relationship with various terrorist groups, including the al-Qaeda organization."

Again and again during the hour-long interview, Cheney said of the Iraqi people: "They will welcome us as liberators."

This was Cheney at the peak of his power, revealing, as he had only briefly on September 11 and during the days that followed, that he was fully in charge. He had the plan, and he had the power to implement it. And for every sincere concern that might be expressed, he had a false promise at the ready. As the interview progressed, Cheney made fewer mentions of President Bush. He kept saying "we." With the hour winding down, there were no longer any mentions of Bush and that "we" was sounding more and more royal. Finally, Russert asked whether fiscal sense might argue for suspending a proposed tax cut for the rich in order to pay for the war. "We don't believe that's the right course of action, Tim. This is one of those times when, as important as the war on terror is and as important as the problem of Iraq is, we've also got a lot of other balls in the air," Cheney said. "And an American president these days doesn't have the choice of focusing on only one thing."

Dick Cheney was, by now, the Machiavelli of his age, having beaten his only serious rival, the pretender Rumsfeld, for a place at the elbow of a boy king who would ever defer to his regent. Yet Cheney had never bothered to develop the knowledge, or the ability to honestly assess information, that would have allowed him to rule wisely. The fatal flaw in Cheney's schemes had turned out to be Cheney. Thirty-four years after he had arrived in Washington as barely an intern, he had made himself the most powerful man in that city and the world beyond. He had the authority to decide between peace and war, and he had chosen war—not because it was necessary, but because it satisfied his needs, politically, economically, and emotionally. Now, people would die—soldiers, contractors, civilians. The violence would, over time, swell. Those who were supposed to greet Americans as liberators would take up arms. And the promise of greater security from terrorism, which Cheney had made with such assurance, would come to be seen as the absurd boast of a man so desperate to begin a war that he never stopped to consider its consequences.

There would need to be an accounting. And in the spring of 2004, it was demanded.

Having heard Richard Clarke's charge that the administration had been more obsessed with regime change in Iraq than with taking the necessary steps to combat terrorism—which was, again, surfacing in the form of bombings that had left more than two hundred Spaniards dead—the members of the National Commission on Terrorist Attacks on the United States had prevailed upon the president to meet with them in secret. But the president would not appear on his own; he would come with Dick Cheney at his side.

It was a necessary pairing. White House aides acknowledged, and the commission accepted, that George W. Bush could not provide answers to the most basic questions about the rationale for the war on Iraq, let alone how it related to the war on terrorism. Iraq was not his project. He was, to be sure, responsible, as the war had been waged in his name. But how could he explain that which he had not conceived and never seemed to fully understand? For that, the commission would need to hear from Dick Cheney.

Of all the powers afforded to the man who occupies the Oval Office, none is more awesome than the authority to lead the most powerful nation in the world to war. Yet George W. Bush, who had campaigned for president as a reluctant warrior who did not want to be the world's policeman, had only placed a seal of approval on another man's plan to launch a preemptive war against a distant land. This was not Bush's war, this was Cheney's war. And because of that, this was not George W. Bush's presidency. It was Dick Cheney's.

When schoolchildren go to the backs of their American history books, they encounter charts that list the presidents and vice presidents of the United States. But the facts of America's decision to go to war with Iraq in the spring of 2003 made a lie of those charts. And history itself is threatened.

So let it be recorded here that, in the first years of the twenty-first century, at a time when American faith in itself had been shaken, the White House became a place of dark and dangerous intrigues. The Oval Office was occupied by a weak and disengaged president in name only. But the authority of the presidency, up to and including the power to plan and wage war, was gripped by an unrelentingly ambitious yet tragically ill-prepared man named Richard Bruce Cheney.

Dick. The man who is president.

A NOTE ON SOURCES

I always felt it was important to have somebody around here who isn't writing a book.

—Dick Cheney, 2004

There is a joke told among those who know Dick Cheney well. It is said that Cheney is always in a secure undisclosed location—even when he is sitting right next to you. The point is well taken. Cheney is, in the words of one *Washington Post* profiler, "ever wary" about revealing any more of himself than he absolutely must. As former congressman Lee Hamilton, who worked closely with Cheney during the Iran-contra hearings of the late 1980s and who more recently questioned the vice president as a member of the National Commission on Terrorist Attacks on the United States, says, "Dick's preference was always to deal quietly, not in public."

Dick Cheney understands that there is power in living an unexamined life. Thus, as a man for whom the accumulation of power is a life mission, Cheney has been meticulous about maintaining an uncommonly low profile. He has always wanted to shape history itself, not be the subject of contemporary books.

Cheney brags about the fact that he does not write books. Less ambitious political figures—Bill Clinton, Colin Powell, John McCain, Rudy Giuliani—pen tell-all tales and confide in celebrity journalists. In so doing, they slowly lose the confidence of official Washington. But Cheney makes no such error. He is unwilling to peddle the secrets of power—be they his own or those of the men he has served as White House chief of staff, secretary of defense, or vice president. In 2004, while leading a tour of his West Wing office, Cheney announced, "Sometimes I think I got this job because I didn't write about the last job." At a time when former cabinet members, White House aides, and well-connected journalists were publishing a shelf of books that seemed to confirm vice presidential historian Timothy Welch's observation that Cheney's authority was "without precedent," the vice president grumbled, "I always felt it was important to have somebody around here who isn't writing a book. And darn near everybody is."

"He's taken on the role of a 'confidence man,' following in a tradition of people who have served presidents discreetly," explains presidential historian Douglas Brinkley. "Cheney's taken discretion to a new art form—that's been one of his primary strengths." And when a powerful man has secrets to keep, he will find no better co-conspirators than the political press corps of Washington, which willingly performs stenography to power in return for the promise of a good seat at the press briefing. As a result, Cheney is well into his fourth decade as the Washington insider about whom remarkably little is known and even less is revealed.

When I first started collecting materials on Dick Cheney, at the time when he was preparing to seek the 1996 Republican presidential nomination, I was amazed by the lack of written material regarding the man. Far less significant figures had their names on file folders full of profiles and news clippings. But Cheney had succeeded in maintaining the lowest of low profiles. Even the people who "know" him note that Cheney is not forthcoming about his feelings or anything more than the collection of sound bites and anecdotes that fill out one of the most comically self-serving official biographies since Joe McCarthy dubbed himself "Tailgunner Joe."

Piecing together the real story of Dick Cheney took time and patience. In preparing this book, I went out of my way to talk with the people who watched Cheney clawing his way up to the first rung on that ladder of success. On the floor of the 2000 Republican National

Convention in Philadelphia, I spent a lovely evening conversing with the bored delegates from Wyoming as they awaited the speech by a "favorite son" whom most of them admitted they did not know very well. I tracked down Cheney's favorite college professor, fellow students, and men who supervised the glorified internships that got him his start in politics. I talked with a lot of Republicans, including some who served with him in Congress, who clashed with him during his tenure as secretary of defense, and who made sure that he did not become their party's candidate for president in 1996. I covered Cheney a bit before his 1996 campaign fizzled and a bit more in 2000. After Cheney returned to Washington in 2001, I found myself keeping an increasingly close eye on him. For *In These Times,* I wrote a major piece on Cheney's attempts to use energy policy to divide the labor-environmentalist alliance that had developed after the 1999 anti–World Trade Organization protests in Seattle. For the *Nation,* I wrote several pieces examining his links to Enron CEO Ken Lay. And as the war with Iraq approached, I found myself writing and commenting on the vice president with increasing frequency. Once, after an appearance on Phil Donahue's old MSNBC program, I got a call from the vice president's office; his press secretary was concerned that I had mentioned business dealings between Halliburton and the Iraqi government of dictator Saddam Hussein, and she said Cheney wanted me to know that he had been a critic of easing sanctions against Iraq. I suggested that the vice president might want to do a detailed interview regarding the subject; it was never scheduled. I have enjoyed several brief conversations with Cheney over the years, however, including the discussion regarding his time spent on the staff of former congressman Bill Steiger that is recounted in chapter 3 of this book.

Ultimately, however, I wanted this book to be grounded in the official record and news reports, a desire that afforded me the opportunity to wade through great stacks of government documents, newspaper articles, and interview transcripts in search of the pieces of Cheney's story. It is important to note that despite his best efforts to avoid the limelight,

Cheney has left a paper trail. It lacks the easy coherence found in the self-serving autobiographies of other powerful players in Washington or in the breathless "insider accounts" penned by White House aides and correspondents who produce gentle renderings of the official story. But, over the years, reporters and authors have pulled the curtain back now and again, as have courageous congressional investigators, most notably California representative Henry Waxman and New Jersey senator Frank Lautenberg. The source notes that follow recognize the work of the journalists and official investigators who have rejected the official spin and searched out the bits and pieces of evidence that tell Cheney's story. My analysis has been informed by their work, as has my confidence that after decades of clawing for personal power, Dick Cheney has not just attained the vice presidency. He has, by aligning himself with a weak "president in name only," made himself the definitional figure in our politics and governance.

INTRODUCTION

The Evil Genius in the Corner

The White House account of the February 7, 2001, shooting incident that is detailed at the opening of this book is a revealing document, which Jake Tapper reviewed with an appropriately skeptical eye in his "Mayhem at the White House" piece for *Salon* (02/08/01). Articles by the *Cincinnati Enquirer,* the *Evansville* (Indiana) *Courier & Press,* and CNN (all from 02/08/01) fill in the details. You can still listen to Cheney's announcement of his selection as the 2000 GOP vice presidential candidate by visiting www.cnn.com/2000/ALLPOLITICS/ stories/07/25/bush.vp, where you'll also find a good written account of the proceedings. Geoff Earle and Stephen Norton did a good review of the early stages of the transition process, where the vice president–elect put his stamp on the new administration, "Cheney Takes Transition

Effort to Capitol Hill," for *CongressDaily* (12/14/00), while Dana Milbank's *Washington Post* piece "The Chairman and the CEO: In Incoming Corporate White House, Bush Is Seen Running Board, Cheney Effecting Policy" (12/24/00) provides an exceptionally useful analysis.

The Center for Responsive Politics report *Returning the Favor: President-Elect Bush's Advisory Teams Include Big Campaign Donors* (01/02/01) provides insights into the money-in-politics side of the story. And, of course, Ron Suskind's *The Price of Loyalty: George W. Bush, the White House and the Education of Paul O'Neill* (Simon & Schuster: 2004) provides fabulous insights regarding Cheney's domineering role in the process of shaping the administration. Howard Fineman's pre-9/11 piece on the problems faced by the Bush administration, "Unsettled Scores," appeared in *Newsweek* magazine (09/17/01). Of the many accounts of Cheney's "take-charge moment" on 9/11, Sharon Otterman's for United Press International (09/07/02) is outstanding, while the detailed review of events in the opening chapter of Richard Clarke's *Against All Enemies* (Free Press: 2004) is useful. James Mann's observations, which to my mind are among the best available regarding this administration, can be found in his essential book *Rise of the Vulcans: The History of the Bush War Cabinet* (Viking: 2004). The "evil genius" line comes from an interview published in *USA Today* under the title "Cheney Says It's Too Soon to Tell on Iraqi Arms" (01/19/04).

CHAPTER 1

Dressed Up Like a Cowboy

Begin any examination of Cheney's upbringing at the official White House Web site (www.whitehouse.gov/vicepresident), where you will find images of the vice president attempting to grip a football and holding up a T-shirt from the Natrona County High School Mustangs and the predictable story. Then, start working toward something more closely akin to the truth. The article on the efforts of Cheney and Rove to divide labor and environmental groups, "Teamsters, Not Turtles: Bush's Strategy to Divide the Democrats," appeared in *In These Times* (06/25/01). Some of the best insights regarding Wyoming in general can be found in Gretel Ehrlich's books, especially *The Solace of Open Spaces* (Viking Penguin: 1985), and the Works Projects Administration's *Wyoming: A Guide to Its History, Highways, and People* (originally published in 1940, reprinted by the University of Nebraska Press in 1981). T. A. Larson's *History of Wyoming* (University of Nebraska Press: 1990) is also quite good, while Don Pitcher's *Wyoming* (Avalon: 2003) provides an outstanding overview. Tom Turnipseed's *The Wild West of Dick Cheney* (Common Dreams: 03/23/01) scopes out the energy issues of the region.

Insights regarding Cheney's family background can be garnered from Phil McCombs's piece "The Unsettling Calm of Dick Cheney" (04/03/91) and Mark Leibovich's "The Strong, Silent Type" (01/18/04), both published in the *Washington Post*, as well as James Carney's "Clues to Understanding Dick Cheney," which appeared in *Time* magazine (12/22/02). A 1985 article for the *Omaha World-Herald*, "Where Are They Now? Nebraska Native Serves Wyoming" (10/20/85), filled out the picture, as did various Cheney/Cheyney family genealogies.

For more on the Soil Conservation movement, visit the Natural Resources Conservation Service web site (www.nrcs.usda.gov/about/history/). Several articles on Cheney's Yale years are revealing, especially Charles Forelle's "Dick Cheney and Yale: An Ill-Suited Match (*Yale Daily News:* 09/09/00), Matthew Ferraro's "From Old Campus to the Oval Office" (*Yale Herald:* 02/07/03), and "Yale Holds Tie to Presidency" (*Boston Globe:* 02/16/04). For insights on Cheney's views regarding H. Bradford Westerfield's classes at Yale, check out Glenn Kessler and Peter Slevin's "Cheney Is Fulcrum of Foreign Policy: In Intragency Fights, His Views Often Prevail" (*Washington Post:* 10/13/02).

Readers can learn a lot about Rock Springs from Don Pitcher's *Wyoming* and from a great article by Paul Krza, "What Dick Cheney

Might Have Learned in Rock Springs, Wyoming" (*High Plains News:* 12/09/02). Cheney's drunk driving record is discussed in Bob Woodward's book *The Commanders* (Simon & Schuster: 1991), and the documents are on display for all to see at www.thesmokinggun.com, along with a quick summary of "Dick Cheney's Youthful Indiscretions." Cheney's return to academia is covered in Carney's *Time* piece and McCombs's *Washington Post* article. And the story of his development of political ties to Wyoming's Republican establishment can be found in a number of articles written around the time of his infrequent returns to the state for political purposes. An especially useful article, "Just So Wyoming," by Chris George appeared in the *Wyoming Tribune-Eagle* (02/26/02), as did Lara Azar's "Cheney Rallies Republicans" (11/04/02) and Becky Orr's "Deal with Iraq—VP" (09/28/02) and "Demonstrators Protest Possible War in Iraq" (09/28/02). Lou Cannon's article "From the White House to the Hustings: Richard Cheney Looks to the Hill" (*Washington Post:* 10/16/78) provided useful insights regarding Cheney's return to Wyoming in 1978, as did T.R. Reid's "Republican Candidates Thrive in Rich, Uncluttered Wyoming" (*Washington Post:* 08/29/78). Glen Johnson's *Boston Globe* piece "Early Knack for Leading Put Cheney on Fast Track" (07/26/00) provides a good basic summary of the material.

Lynne Cheney's notes to the Colorado College Alumni Office, which detail the family's Texas residency, are contained in the school's "Class Notes" releases. *The Dallas Morning News* (09/08/00) detailed Cheney's Texas voting record in the article "Bush's Running Mate Skipped 14 Elections in Five Years," while several *Austin American Statesman* articles (11/22/00) reviewed Cheney's use of tax breaks available only to Texas residents. The Associated Press provided solid coverage of the challenge to Cheney's Wyoming residency claim in articles such as "Texans Challenge Cheney's Residency Status" (11/21/00). A *Washington Post* op-ed piece by Philip Bobbitt and Stuart Taylor Jr., "An Amended Administration" (11/27/00), laid out the legal case on the residency issue.

Ski magazine's "Jackson Hole's VIP" (02/04) provides not just anecdotes, but fun photos of "the first sitting U.S. Vice President to live in
a ski town," although it never strays beyond the agreed-upon topic:
"Cheney's connection to skiing." The Associated Press's "In Jackson,
Wyo., Cheney Blends In" (12/23/00) provides more information, as
does Jessica Lowell's *Wyoming Tribune-Eagle* piece "When Planes Land,
It's Not Much of a Secret Anymore" (08/16/03). Finally, Jackson Hole
resident Nathaniel Burt's book is a treasure, and he offers insights regarding Cheney's lifestyle in his *Compass American Guide to Wyoming*
(Random House: 2002).

CHAPTER 2

Deferred Patriotism

David Maraniss's marvelous book *They Marched into Sunlight* (Simon &
Schuster: 2003) provides a good deal of information regarding Cheney's
detached approach to the 1960s, and conversations with the author
added insight. Reports on Cheney's Senate confirmation hearings for
the position of secretary of defense and his tenure in that position provided basic information about his draft avoidance. Phil McCombs of
the *Washington Post* was one of the first writers to take a serious look at
Cheney's draft record; his 1991 piece "The Unsettling Calm of Dick
Cheney" (04/03/91) contains a particularly thoughtful review of the
facts and sound analysis. But the story of Cheney's deferments really
took off after Cheney selected himself as Bush's running mate. *Salon's*
Jake Tapper was on the story early, with an aggressive piece, "Ex-
Clinton Official Slams Bush and Cheney War Records" (08/01/2000),
that provided a great review of former secretary of veterans affairs
Jesse Brown's views regarding Cheney. Other writers worked parts of
the story over the years, including *Slate's* Timothy Noah ("Elizabeth
Cheney, Deferment Baby": 03/18/04). But few have done more with

the material than Vietnam vet Dennis Mansker, whose Web site (www.dennismansker.com) refers to the president and vice president as "the two Chief Chickenhawks" and examines the question "Who died in your place, Dick Cheney?" The *New York Times* finally picked up on the story in 2004, with Katharine Q. Seelye's article (05/01/04) "Cheney's Five Draft Deferments During the Vietnam Era Emerge as a Campaign Issue."

The University of Wisconsin's University Communications Office helpfully provided what materials they could regarding Cheney's sprint through the campus, and they were useful, although conversations with his fellow students and members of the faculty proved to be more revealing. Cheney spoke with the *Milwaukee Journal*'s Steve Walters about his work with former governor Warren Knowles ("Cheney Tours Wisconsin, Calls for New Military Vigor": 10/13/00). The files of the *Capital Times* newspaper in Madison, Wisconsin, provided details about the Knowles years, as did conversations with former Knowles aides. Those same files also provided a great deal of perspective on Representative Bill Steiger, as did conversations with many of Steiger's friends in Wisconsin and with the vice president. When Bill Steiger's wife, Janet, died in 2004, I wrote a lengthy reflection of the couple that examined his moderate politics, "Steigers Shone Brightly on Political Scene" (*Capital Times:* 04/08/04).

CHAPTER 3

Dick Rising

No one wrote more ably about Donald Rumsfeld than the late Steve Neal, whose articles and columns for the *Chicago Tribune* and *Chicago Sun-Times* provided the best insights regarding the man's accomplishments and ambitions. Two good examples of Neal's writing are his 1985 *Tribune* piece "Rumsfeld Almost Off and Running" (04/04/85), in which he explored the prospects for a Rumsfeld presidential run in 1988, and a related 1986 *Chicago Tribune* magazine piece, "Donald Rumsfeld Gets Down to the Business of Running for President" (01/26/86). Carol Felsenthal's "The Don," which appeared in *Chicago magazine* in June 2001, is filled with useful information. Gerald Ford aide Robert T. Hartmann's book *Palace Politics* (McGraw-Hill: 1980) is necessary reading, as is Ron Nessen's *It Sure Looks Different from the Inside* (Playboy Paperbacks: 1978) and H. R. Haldeman's *The Haldeman Diaries* (G.P. Putnam: 1994) and John Ehrlichman's *Witness to Power* (Simon & Schuster: 1982). Among contemporary texts, Bob Woodward's *Bush at War* (Simon & Schuster: 2002) is somewhat useful, while James Mann's *Rise of the Vulcans* is a treasure trove of information and able analysis. Mann's *Atlantic* magazine piece "Close Up: Young Rumsfeld" (11/03) pulls the material together brilliantly. The able Jason Vest wrote a pair of great pieces, "Darth Rumsfeld" and "Punch-Drunk on Hardball: Online Sidebar to 'Darth Rumsfeld,' " for the *American Prospect* magazine and its Web site (02/26/01). While the story of the development of Cheney's relationship with Rumsfeld has been told in many ways, my conversations with people who knew Bill Steiger have tended to confirm the story line that Mann has developed. The Steiger files at the *Capital Times* are packed with background information about the congressman's remarkable career. I also found a good many useful articles in files from the old *Milwaukee Sentinel* and *Journal* newspapers, which covered Steiger closely.

My colleague and friend Bruce Shapiro was one of the first writers to explore the history of Rumsfeld and Cheney as Nixon-era hipsters, with his fine piece "Restoring the Imperial Presidency" for *Salon* (06/17/02). Additionally, Shapiro's piece examined the penchant of Cheney toward secrecy and unchecked power, a subject explored by Stephen Pizzo in his piece "Nixon's Children" for TomPaine.com (02/12/04). John Dean's www.findlaw.com article "The Nixon Shadow That Hovers over the Bush White House" (01/06/03) accurately portrays Cheney as a true heir to Tricky Dick's worst legacies. But the best confirmation of all may come in the transcripts of Cheney's remarks when he appeared at the Richard Nixon Library and Birthplace (02/19/02).

New Republic writer John Osborne's "White House Watch" columns provide the best history of the Rumsfeld–Cheney dark side of the Ford White House. They are collected in his good book *White House Watch: The Ford Years* (New Republic Books: 1977). Osborne's long review of Robert Hartmann's *Palace Politics* for the *New York Times* (08/10/80), "Nice Guy with Villains," provides additional insight into the intrigues involving Nelson Rockefeller. Cheney's own comments about battling Rockefeller, delivered during a 1986 University of California symposium involving former White House chiefs of staff, are incredibly revealing. They were published in a *Washington Monthly* article titled "Tales from the Top: Eight Former Chiefs of Staff Reflect," by Samuel Kernell and Samuel L. Popkin (04/87). More tidbits can be found in Ed Walsh's *Washington Post* piece "Central Role for Jordan" (02/22/77).

Lou Cannon's book *Governor Reagan: His Rise to Power* (Public Affairs: 2003) offers a good perspective on the fight for the 1976 Republican nomination in general and on Reagan's prodding of the Ford team in particular. Cheney's memorandums from the campaign make for interesting reading; they are found at the University of Texas, with some available online at www.ford.utexas.edu/library/exhibits/cheney.htm. State-by-state results from the 1976 general election can be found online at www.multied.com/elections/1976state.html. There are a number of good biographies and biographical papers that deal with Nelson Rockefeller. I found the review of Rockefeller's vice presidency on the Web at www.allamericanpatriots.com to be thorough and extremely useful, particularly in its examination of Ford's regret at having dropped Rockefeller from the ticket.

The Reuters report on the Cheney–Scalia controversy, "Justice Scalia Refuses to Recuse in Cheney Case" (03/18/04), provides a good basic review of the issues involved. Another useful piece, "The Justice,

His VP Friend, and Questions," by David Ballingrud appeared in the *St. Petersburg Times* (02/17/04). For a more detailed review of the issues surrounding the question of recusal by Supreme Court justices, see *Jews for Buchanan* (New Press: 2001). The federal law on recusal can be found in the statute books at 28 USC 455.

CHAPTER 4

Apartheid's Congressman

Nelson Mandela's statements regarding Cheney come from interviews conducted with him in the United States and South Africa and from an interview he did with *Newsweek* ("Nelson Mandela: The USA Is a Threat to World Peace," *Newsweek* Web Exclusive: 09/10/02) and BBC News reports (09/11/02). Joe Conason's fine piece for *Salon,* "Dick Cheney Is Relying on Our Cultural Amnesia to Wipe Away His Record on South Africa" (08/01/00), puts things in perspective, as does the transcript from the PBS *NewsHour* program "The Politics of Dick Cheney" (07/26/00).

The *NewsHour* transcript also provides a good overview of the official reaction to Cheney's selection as George W. Bush's running mate, although a more typical report, "Former House Mate Likes Cheney for Veep," from Pennsylvania's *Northeast Times* (08/02/00), offers telling evidence of how frequently Cheney is mischaracterized as a moderate. The story of Cheney's own determination to avoid that characterization has been repeated in several contexts, including James Carney's *Time* article "Clues to Understanding Dick Cheney" and James Mann's book *Rise of the Vulcans.* Bob Jones's analysis of Cheney's congressional voting record for the conservative *World* magazine (08/05/00) celebrates Cheney as "a solid, all-around conservative," while Cheney's remarks in a 2004 speech at the Ronald Reagan Presidential Library (03/17/04) make the same point. Skip Oliva's "Cheney: On the

'Right' Track" provides a more critical analysis (generationvote.com: 09/02/00). The *Congressional Quarterly Almanacs* for the years of Cheney's congressional service are the best source for details regarding his voting record. Reviews of Cheney's record by People for the American Way and the Sierra Club (especially the *Cheney Pick Would Be Threat to the Environment* report: 07/24/00) provided good background material. *Business Week*'s comparison of Cheney and Jesse Helms appeared in the 03/02/98 issue. Newt Gingrich was quoted in several contexts suggesting that Cheney had a more conservative congressional record, including a 07/25/00 *Washington Times* article.

For background on Teno Roncalio, visit the www.roncalio.com Web site or check out the quite good *Empire* magazine profile "Teno Roncalio: Wyoming Whirlwind" (04/14/63). A good obituary, "Former Rep. Teno Roncalio, Wyoming Democrat, Dies at 87," appeared in the *Wyoming Tribune-Eagle* (04/03/03). For background on the remarkable Joseph O'Mahoney, begin with the *Biographical Directory of the United States Congress.* The Wyoming secretary of state's office provided a useful roster of U.S. senators and representatives for the state and their partisan affiliations. As noted before, Lou Cannon's reporting on the 1978 House race for the *Washington Post* was very useful. Phil McCombs's 1991 piece for the *Post,* "The Unsettling Calm of Dick Cheney" (04/03/91), offered insights regarding Cheney's willingness to use his heart condition as a political tool. The Congressional Quarterly Voting and Elections Collection (CQ Electronic Library) provides background on Cheney's margins of victory, while the Center for Public Integrity's reports on Cheney from "The Buying of the Presidency 2004" (www.bop2004.org) detail the campaign contributions he collected.

Dick and Lynne Cheney's book on Speakers of the House is *Kings of the Hill* (Touchstone: 1983). Lynne Cheney's book *Sisters* was published in 1981 by New American Library and is, sadly, out of print. Laura Flanders, author of the excellent book *Bushwomen: Tales of a Cynical Species* (Verso Books: 2004), has done much to bring it to public at-

tention. Associated Press covered the controversy about the book's proposed republication, "U.S. Vice President's Wife Stops Reissue of Sexy
Novel She Wrote in 1981" (04/02/04). Background on the flap over
the faux bio of Lynne can be found at the exceptionally witty
www.whitehouse.org Web site. The controversy over Cheney's evolving stance on same-sex marriage has been well detailed. One particularly useful piece, "Robertson Defends Statement That God Says
Bush Will Be Re-elected," appeared in the *Virginian-Pilot* (02/02/04);
another, "Gays Demand That Cheney's Daughter Oppose Bush," was
published by the *Chicago Tribune* (03/07/04). Michelangelo Signorile's
"Dear Mary" letter appeared in the *New York Press* (01/20/2004), and
the www.dearmary.com Web site picks up the story from there.

John Dean's essays on Cheney's push to consolidate power in the
executive branch are essential reading. You'll find them at http://writ
.news.findlaw.com/dean/. Some of the best writing regarding Cheney's
role in the Iran-Contra hearings and their aftermath can be found in the
archives of the *Christian Science Monitor*. Look especially at Peter Oster-
lund's "GOP congressman warns against limiting presidential power"
(*Christian Science Monitor,* 11/24/87). Read, also, George Lardner Jr.'s
"GOP Minority Denounces Panel Findings as 'Hysterical' " (*Washington Post,* 11/19/97). Philip Shenon's article, "GOP Iran Contra Report
Defends President" (*New York Times,* 11/16/87) has lots of fine quotes
and good background information, as does the late great Mary Mc-
Grory's "Boxed in By the Iran Reports" (*Washington Post,* 11/24/87).
For details of the Cheney-Poindexter exchange, see "Poindexter Ex-
presses No Regrets" by Walter Pincus and Dan Morgan (*Washington
Post,* 7/21/87). A comparative reading of the Majority and Minority
Reports of the Congressional Iran-Contra Committees yields a good
deal of insight regarding Cheney's role and his ideas. For more on Che-
ney's role during the 1991 Gulf War, and his attitudes toward consulting
Congress, see Bob Woodward's *The Commanders.* Woodward's *Plan of
Attack* offers some insight regarding consultation with Congress prior
to the Iran invasion. Quotes from members of Congress are from the

Congressional record and statements released by their offices, as well as reports on the debate produced by the author for *The Nation*.

CHAPTER 5

Pocketing the Peace Dividend

A quite thorough, if not always skeptical, review of Cheney's service as secretary of defense can be found on the Web at www.defenselink.mil. Bob Woodward's 1991 book, *The Commanders,* and Richard Clarke's *Against All Enemies* from 2004 provide some useful background on Cheney's service at the Pentagon. But Chalmers Johnson's *The Sorrows of Empire* (Metropolitan Books: 2004) is the must-read on the subject. Johnson's brilliant analysis continually informs my views, as it does those of many others. Jane Mayer's *New Yorker* article "Contract Sport" (02/16–23/04) is filled with important information and insights, as are several articles from the time of Cheney's departure from the House to join the first Bush administration. One of the best was David Hoffman's "Rep. Cheney Chosen as Defense Nominee" (*Washington Post:* 03/11/89); the *Post's* coverage of Cheney's confirmation hearings was the most thorough and useful. The transcript of the press conference at which Cheney's nomination was announced, available from the Bush Library, is helpful. I also turned to Stephen Hess's "First Impressions: A Look Back at Five Presidential Transitions" (*Brookings Review:* spring 2001).

David Rosenbaum's *New York Times* article "From Guns to Butter" (12/14/89) gives insights into the "peace dividend" debate, as does a Michael Putzel article from the *Boston Globe,* "Battle Joined on 'Peace Dividend' " (01/12/92). An *Army Times* interview with Colin Powell, "Powell: I'm Running Out of Demons" (04/05/91), offers additional insights. Dana Milbank's *Washington Post* piece "The Chairman and the CEO: In Incoming Corporate White House, Bush Is Seen Running

Board, Cheney Effecting Policy" (12/24/00) offers the proper contemporary perspective on Cheney's manipulation of the debate and the Congress.

Cheney's speeches to the American Enterprise Institute are revealing with regard to his views, especially his address of 02/21/91, and a lengthy speech he gave as he prepared to seek the 1996 Republican presidential nomination, "Getting Our Priorities Right" (12/08/93), is revealing. "Defense Strategy for the 1990s: The Regional Defense Startegy," the plan that Cheney submitted in January 1993, is available from the Pentagon and makes for chilling reading in light of later developments. Good reporting on the development of the document was done by Patrick Tyler of the *New York Times,* whose articles, "U.S. Strategy Plan Calls for Insuring No Rivals Develop" (03/08/92) and "Pentagon Drops Goal of Blocking New Superpowers" (05/24/92), provide basic background, as does Barton Gellman's "Keeping the U.S. First: Pentagon Would Preclude a Rival Superpower" (*Washington Post:* 03/11/92). James Mann, who wrote several analytical articles on these issues at the time, brings the analysis up-to-date in *Rise of the Vulcans.*

Also, the extensive oral history that Cheney did for PBS's *Frontline* program "The Gulf War" is a revealing and useful document. It can be found on the Web at www.pbs.org.

George Bush explained his reading habits—or lack thereof—to Fox News anchor Brit Hume in a 9/22/03 interview on the program "Special Report." The transcript is worth reading; it's at http://www.foxnews.com/story/0,2933,98111,00.html. Also recommended is Helen Thomas's scathing review of the interview, "No wonder Bush doesn't connect with the rest of the country" (UPI: 10/15/03). Cheney's remarks on the quality of post–9/11 journalism were made at a March 6, 2004 Gridiron dinner in Washington. The vice president's comments on Fox can be found in the article, "Cheney Praises Fox News Channel," by *Washington Post* writer Mike Allen (4/30/04). Details about the firing of General Michael J. Dugan can be found in *Christian Science Monitor* writer Francine Kiefer's article "Cheney Again

Walks Mideast High Wire" (3/8/02). A good basic review of the Adam Clymer "big time" flap was done by the Associated Press in the article, "Bush Uses Profanity About Reporter" (9/4/2000). In his article, "The Hersh Alternative," Bob Thompson of the *Washington Post* produced a good summary of Cheney's consideration of plans to "muzzle" Seymour Hersh during the Ford years (1/28/01). AP's Doug Simpson reported on the veep's speech to newspaper editors regarding Iraq coverage and the killing of journalists in a piece titled, "Cheney Says War Criticism Is Misguided" (4/9/03). David Carr of the *New York Times* reported on Cheney's distribution of the *Weekly Standard* at the White House (3/12/03).

CHAPTER 6

CEO of the U.S.A.

The Center for Public Integrity has been all over the Cheney-Halliburton story, publishing excellent reports such as *Cheney Led Halliburton to Feast at Federal Trough* (02/07/04), while organizations such as CorpWatch and Citizen Works have done great work in this area. U.S. representative Henry Waxman and U.S. senator Frank Lautenberg have been champions in the struggle to reveal the details of Cheney's dealings, as well as those of other Halliburton officials. Texas journalist Robert Bryce was one of the first to seriously examine the full history of Cheney's official dealings with Halliburton's Brown & Root subsidiary; his article "The Candidate from Brown & Root" (*Austin Chronicle*: 08/28/00) is essential reading, as is Jane Mayer's *New Yorker* Letter from Washington piece "Contract Sport" (02/16–23/04). I would also recommend Frida Berrigan's "Halliburton's Axis of Influence" (*In These Times*: 3/28/03). The *Washington Post* maintains "A Halliburton Primer" at its Web site, www.washingtonpost.com, which reviews some of the more serious controversies involving the company.

A basic history of Halliburton can be found at www.halliburton.com, along with many of the company's press releases from over the years. Former Halliburton CEO Tom Cruikshank's remarkably frank comments about why Cheney was hired can be found in Laurence McQuillan's revealing *USA Today* article "Prying into Cheney's Business" (06/10/02). McQuillan's article also provides useful details regarding the Dresser merger. *Business Week's* "The Cheney Question" (07/12/02) provides information regarding corporate accountability and accounting controversies involving Halliburton. A BBC report, "Cheney Accused of Corporate Fraud" (07/10/02), is also useful. The nominee for most revealing headline, however, goes to a 2000 article by CNNfn staff writer Chris Isidore that appeared on the day Cheney's selection as a vice presidential nominee was announced: "VP Pick Credited with Halliburton's Revival: Company Future Seen as Secure" (07/25/00).

Henry Waxman's dogged inquiries into accusations of war profiteering by Halliburton are detailed on his official Web site, www.house.gov/waxman, and conversations with him for articles that appeared in the *Nation* were exceptionally educational. Pratap Chatterjee's "Halliburton Makes a Killing on Iraq War" (www.corpwatch.org: 03/20/03) is very useful, as is Citizen Works' "Dick Cheney and Halliburton: A Chronology," which can be found at www.citizenworks.org, along with a fine article, "Cheney, Halliburton and the Spoils of War," by Lee Drutman and Charlie Cray. For more on the failure of most major media to cover the Bush administration in an aggressive manner, see Bob McChesney's *The Problem of the Media* (Monthly Review Press: 2004).

John Judis penned a great report of Cheney's China wheeling and dealing, "Chinatown" (03/10/97), for the *New Republic.* The *Washington Post* has been in the forefront of examining Halliburton's links to Saddam Hussein's government, with articles going back to 2000. A good review of the information can be found in the article "Halliburton's Iraq Deals Greater Than Cheney Has Said" (06/23/01), by Colum Lynch. The *San Francisco Bay Guardian's* Martin A. Lee was on the story early with a piece titled "Cheney Made Millions Off Oil Deals with Hussein" (11/13/00). Among major dailies, the *Post* has done a better job than most when it comes to examining potential Cheney-Halliburton scandals, although their headline writing leaves something to be desired. The *Post's* 02/10/04 story "Cheney, a Little Tarnished" actually contains useful information about some of the controversies swirling around Halliburton's international dealings, as does a *New York Times* piece from the same period, "Halliburton Likely to Be a Campaign Issue This Fall" (02/14/04). But the best accounting of the issues can often be found in progressive publications and alternative newsweeklies. The *Boston Phoenix's* Dan Kennedy has produced a fine report on legal issues arising from Halliburton's African dealings during Cheney's tenure, "Dick Cheney's Nigerian Nightmare" (02/27/04). Doug Ireland writing in the *Nation* (12/29/03) is excellent on this subject. The Center for Public Integrity's *Cheney Led Halliburton to Feast at Federal Trough* is the essential document regarding Export-Import Bank issues. My conversations with U.S. representative Bernie Sanders for several *Nation* pieces were also terrifically helpful. One of those articles, "Enron's Global Crusade" (03/04/02), discusses Cheney's activities at some length.

The Cheney-Enron link is explored in this writer's piece "Enron: What Dick Cheney Knew" (the *Nation:* 04/15/02) and in several very good *San Francisco Chronicle* reports, including "Memo Details Cheney-Enron Links" (01/30/02) and "Boxer, Feinstein Seize on 'Smoking Gun' Note" (01/31/02).

CHAPTER 7

Unnatural Selection

For more on the Bush family's concerns about George's ability to assume the presidency, see *Shrub: The Short but Happy Political Life of George*

W. Bush (Random House: 2000), by Molly Ivins and Louis DuBose, and the chapter "Bushwhacked by the Better Brother" in *Jews for Buchanan* (New Press, 2001). Details regarding the embarrassing "pop quiz" incident can be found in "Bush Fumbles Reporter's Pop Quiz" (*USA Today:* 11/05/99). For a good assessment of Rumsfeld's desire to be the vice president, see Carol Felsenthal's "The Don" (*Chicago* magazine: 06/01). James Klurfeld's wise analysis of the Bush family's intention's regarding Cheney, "Put the Blame on Cheney for U.S. Mess in Iraq," appeared 12/08/03 in *Newsday*. The details of Bush's initial conversations with Cheney come from Bush's own statements, including his 07/25/00 announcement of Cheney's selection for the ticket. Information about the selection process, particularly the closing stages of it, were best recorded in the daily summary stories that appeared on CNN's news programs. They are archived at the www.cnn.com's AllPolitics Web site, where readers will find the key quotes and comments revealing the skepticism of top Republicans about Cheney's motives and actions. The *New York Times,* the *Washington Post* and the *Dallas Morning News* also provided good running commentary. An Associated Press report, "Cheney Cashes in Large Stake in Halliburton Stock" (07/25/00), details the financial side of the arrangement. Another useful AP piece, "Cheney Developed Heart Troubles at Early Age," by science writer Paul Recer was published the same day. For an interesting analysis of the selection from a conservative perspective, see "Why Bush Chose Cheney" (www.enterstageright.com: 07/31/00) by Nicholas Sanchez and Leo K. O'Drudy III, both of whom are associated with the Free Congress Foundation. Examples of the enthusiastic response of right-wing Republicans to Cheney's selection are archived at People for the American Way's Right Wing Watch Online site (www .pfaw.org).

Speeches by Bush and Cheney from the Republican National Convention, as well as some basic background on the selection process, can be found in the Congressional Quarterly Voting and Elections Collection (CQ Electronic Library). Two useful sources on the transition process are Dana Milbank's "The Chairman and the CEO: In Incoming Corporate White House, Bush Is Seen Running Board, Cheney Effecting Policy" (*Washington Post:* 12/24/00) and Ron Suskind's *The Price of Loyalty: George W. Bush, the White House and the Education of Paul O'Neill* (Simon & Schuster: 2004). Again, Stephen Hess's "First Impressions: A Look Back at Five Presidential Transitions" (*Brookings Review:* spring 2001) is valuable for the perspective it provides. Consider, as well, the *Christian Science Monitor's* "Cheney Vice-Presidential Load Is Heaviest Yet" (03/07/01).

Cheney's lead role in setting energy policy has been well documented. U.S. representative Henry Waxman's official Web site pulls together much of the most important information at www.house.gov/waxman, and the materials gleaned by the group Judicial Watch as part of its legal challenge to Cheney's secrecy are significant and useful. Two pieces from the *Financial Times* provide detail and perspective: "Vice President's Decision Increases Chances of Legal Challenge from Congress as It Probes Enron's Fall," by Deborah McGregor (01/28/02), and "Man in the News Dick Cheney: The U.S. Vice President Is a Powerful Figure in George W. Bush's Administration; But Accusations About His Corporate Past Will Test His Ability to Remain Behind the Scenes . . . ," by Gerald Baker (07/13/02). See also "Enron: What Dick Cheney Knew" (the *Nation:* 04/15/02).

Cheney's ties to Karl Rove and his involvement with the judicial selection process are detailed in a number of articles by this writer that have appeared in the *Nation, In These Times,* and other publications. In addition to "Teamsters, Not Turtles: Bush's Strategy to Divide the Democrats" (*In These Times:* 06/25/01), check out "Karl Rove's Legal Triolto" (the *Nation:* 07/03/02) and "Fighting Pickering" (03/18/02). Joshua Micah Marshall's article "Vice Grip: Dick Cheney Is a Man of Principles; Disastrous Principles" (*Washington Monthly:* 1/03) provides many useful insights regarding Cheney's political scheming, as does Ron Suskind's *The Price of Loyalty*. Suskind's earlier article on John DiIulio's memo (*Esquire:* 01/03) is essential reading.

Cheney's political manipulations are hardly a secret, but rarely have they been so appallingly revealed as during the fight to defeat U.S. senator Paul Wellstone. Minnesota Republican Tim Pawlenty described Cheney's pressure on him at a 04/18/01 press conference and in subsequent interviews. I covered the race from start to finish and wrote about the Pawlenty incident in a column for the *Capital Times,* "Bush Fears Tenacious, Popular Wellstone," and several articles for the *Nation* during the course of 2002. The article, "Wellstone Family to Bush: Don't Send Cheney" (*Capital Times:* 10/29/02), explains the feelings of the Wellstone family regarding the vice president. Interviews with Wellstone aides, including campaign manager Jeff Blodgett, as well as Secretary of Health and Human Services Tommy Thompson, who attended the funeral instead of Cheney, fleshed out the story.

CHAPTER 8

Dick Cheney's War

WHDH-TV's report of Andy Hiller's quiz of Bush aired 11/03/99. A transcript can be found at www3.whdh.com under the title "Does George W. Bush Know What It Takes to Be President?" His campaign's defenses of Bush can be found in many articles, including "Bush Fumbles Reporter's Pop Quiz" (*USA Today:* 11/05/99). I spoke with Bush a number of times during the primary season, covered the 2000 campaign from start to finish, and did my share of reports on concerns regarding Bush's abilities, as did every other serious reporter on the trail of the 2000 campaign, but Hiller's "gotcha" report remains the most revealing document. It rattled the campaign and strengthened the hand of Cheney and his allies, as James Mann ably explains in *Rise of the Vulcans.* For more on the Project for the New American Century, visit their Web site at www.newamericancentury.org and read Brian Whitaker's "U.S. Think Tanks Give Lessons in Foreign Policy" (the *Guardian,* London: 08/09/03). The activist Web site www.MoveOn.org provides a good review of the project and its key players in its bulletin section. This chapter relies heavily on the transcripts of the three 2000 presidential debates, as well as reports on those debates, such as Ian Christopher McCaleb's article for www.cnn.com "Even-Keeled Cheney-Lieberman Debate Takes Global View" (10/06/00).

Ron Suskind's *The Price of Loyalty* and Richard Clarke's *Against All Enemies* detail the extent of Cheney's early and ongoing focus on Iraq, as does the very good *Newsweek* cover story "How Dick Cheney Sold the War" (11/17/03). Bob Woodward's *Plan of Attack* makes similar points. The documents released as a result of Judicial Watch's FOIA request include details about the energy task force's interest in Iraqi oil (*Judicial Watch Inc. v. Department of Energy, et al.,* Civil Action No. 01–0981). A review of some of Cheney's more outlandish statements, as well as those of other administration insiders, can be found in "Iraq on the Record: The Bush Administration's Public Statements on Iraq," which was prepared for U.S. representative Henry Waxman by the minority staff of the House Committee on Government Reform (03/16/04). *Vanity Fair's* extensive report "The Path to War: The Ultimate Inside Account" (05/04) does a good job of living up to its title.

Cheney's own interviews and speeches from the period before the start of the war are essential documents, especially the 08/27/02 address to the Veterans of Foreign Wars national convention. The vice president's 12/09/03 introduction of Lady Margaret Thatcher at a Heritage Foundation event is also revealing, as is his 07/24/03 American Enterprise Institute speech, "The Continuing War on Terror." Of course, the most significant of his statements are found in the transcript of the 03/16/03 interview with Tim Russert on NBC's *Meet the Press.* For additional perspective, William Keegan's article "The Overruling of the President" (the *Observer,* London: 0118/04) is very good, as are the *Atlanta Journal-Constitution* editorial "Allegations of Bush Critic Offer Troubling View of Iraq" (03/24/04) and William Neikirk's "Democrats Criticize, Bush Advisers Qualify '16 Words' About Uranium"

(*Chicago Tribune:* 07/13/03). Weapons inspector Scott Ritter's views can be sampled in a *Boston Globe* op-ed from July 20, 2002. Neikirk's article gets into the Joe Wilson case, as does the very good report from Veteran Intelligence Professionals for Sanity, *Intelligence Unglued* (07/14/03). Conversations with Wilson provided a good deal of additional insight.

MSNBC's Chris Matthews has done a better job than anyone else on broadcast and cable television of keeping after Cheney. His *Hardball* interview with Richard Clarke (03/31/04) was a definitive discussion. That it did not become front-page news around the world offers a measure of the failure of most media to get serious about the fundamental issue of who led America into the current war with Iraq.

ACKNOWLEDGMENTS

In the first months of 2004, Dick Cheney came more and more into the spotlight, as serious questions arose regarding the role that his staffers appeared to have played in approving contracts with Halliburton, the corporation Cheney served as CEO, and as the 9-11 Commission asked him to explain why, against all evidence, he continued to claim there were serious linkages between Saddam Hussein's Iraq and Osama bin Laden's al-Qaeda network. But when I first started talking about doing a book on Cheney, only a few people recognized the full significance of examining the activities of the most powerful vice president in American history.

One of them, *New York Daily News* Washington bureau chief Lars-Erik Nelson, could have written a great book on Cheney. He was one of the first journalists to seriously examine the scope of the Bush-Cheney ticket's oil-industry connections, and his aggressive and effective reporting influenced my thinking about the role Cheney would play in the administration. Nelson's untimely death in 2000 was a tragic loss for American journalism, and I wrote this book with him often in mind.

My friend Robert W. McChesney, with whom I have written several books and many articles on media issues, was excited from the start about this project. Bob's understanding of media monopoly issues is well known, but his understanding of politics and economics makes him an unsurpassed analyst of the current crisis, and his good spirit makes him the very best comrade any writer could ever want. Karen Rothmyer, one of my editors at *The Nation,* encouraged me to do a cover story on Cheney's dark dealings early on, as did Craig Aaron, of *In These Times.* Karen's interest, in particular, encouraged me to keep on the Cheney story, and I owe her a debt of gratitude that will not soon be repaid.

My colleague and friend, Meredith Clark, one of the savviest students of contemporary political affairs I know, stepped in to do important research at a critical stage. She came to know Cheney's record as well, and sometimes better than I did. She made this book possible, as did Andrew Hsiao, my editor at The New Press, who kept pressing me to do it even as other assignments and responsibilities arose. Andy's faith and gentle prodding were the essential elements that moved the project from conversations in coffee shops to bookstore shelves. The rest of The New Press crew was fantastic. Special marks to Steve Cupid Theodore, who has several great books in him. Diane Wachtell pushed at precisely the right time; she always does. And I am indebted to Colin Robinson, Maury Botton, and Yevgeniya Nagorny. Special marks to André Schiffrin for a great title suggestion, and a great publishing house. My editor at *The Nation,* Katrina vanden Heuvel, was always flexible and generous with insights and suggestions, as was my editor at the *Capital Times* newspaper in Madison, WI, Dave Zweifel—the best newspaperman in America. A special thank you goes, as well, to my colleague Judy Ettenhofer at the *Capital Times,* who makes everything happen.

I am passionately appreciative of the people who agreed to be interviewed for this book, and of everyone who provided information, insights, skeptical questions, and patriotic calls to action. It would be impossible to thank everyone, and I do apologize for omissions, but I do want to note U.S. Representatives Henry Waxman, Bernie Sanders, Sherrod Brown and Jesse Jackson, Jr.; Brad Westerfield, Joe Wilson, David Maraniss, John Patrick Hunter, John Robinson Block, Midge Miller, Tricia Denker, Paul Soglin, Bill Kraus, Scot Ross, Steve Cobble, Bill Moyers, Studs Terkel, Greg Palast, Arianna Huffington, Ed Garvey, Matt Rothschild, Ruth Conniff, David Austin, Laura Dresser, Fred McKissack, Adam Benedetto, and Mark Pocan. The baristas at Ancora Coffee provided the fuel, while Bob Marley and the Wailers, Toots and the Maytals, Patti Smith, Laura Nyro, Joe Strummer and the Mescaleros, and the North Mississippi Allstars provided the soundtrack.

My parents, Harrison and Mary Nichols, and Mary Bottari offered unlimited intellectual and moral support. Rita Bottari served as a midwife for the delivery of the book. And my great Aunt Carolyn Fry served, as she always does, as my inspiration, in politics and in life. This book is dedicated to the memory of the late U.S. Senator Paul Wellstone and to the future of Whitman Genevieve Bottari Nichols, who I hope and believe will live her life in the world that Wellstone wanted.

John Nichols
June 2004